PLAY

A PATH TO GENIUS

PLAY

A PATH TO GENIUS

Nicole Daedone

soulmaker | PRESS

soulmaker | PRESS

Soulmaker Press
soulmakerpress.com

Copyright © 2023 Soulmaker Press

All rights reserved. No part of this book may be reproduced in
any form without written permission from the publisher.

ISBN: 978-1-961064-09-6 (Paperback)
ISBN: 978-1-961064-10-2 (eBook)

Library of Congress Cataloging-in-Publication Data
Available Upon Request

Printed in the United States of America

Contents

Preface

PLAY IS OUR MOST NATURAL means to engage with the world. The delight and curiosity of our most formative experiences were essential to discovering not only its landscape and the others who exist there, but ourselves as players in the unfolding game. The entire universe, and ourselves in it, came alive in play.

The act of play is, in itself, a celebration of agency. It offers us a break from the scripted realities in which we often find ourselves, allowing us to explore the realm of optionality. Its challenges bring us into a more complete expression of ourselves, and its rewards draw us deeper into our being. We play for the experience of playing, all of its elements contributing to the fun.

However, as we navigate through life, our playfulness slowly becomes confined within rigid boundaries, only allowed in tightly predetermined areas of our life, played for clear and definite outcomes. The childhood games have been decided, the outcomes set, and we find ourselves acting out scripts, forgetting the initial choice to participate in our finite selection of roles and moves. The improvisational dynamism of play is reduced to stale recitation.

But as serious as we may convince ourselves to be, as dire the consequences, as restrictive the obligations, play just won't go away. It winks from the periphery, the option always present to allow our awareness to open, to discover the liberation it offers.

This book invites you to reconsider the concept of play, not as a respite from tedium, but as the fabric that underlies our life and the world around us, connecting us to the depths of our biological being and to the heights of our greatest spiritual experiences. More than an exploration of play and games as a curiosity to be studied, this is a call to action, a plea to reclaim the joy and freedom inherent in a playful universe. It is an opportunity to rediscover the transformative, liberating power of play.

1

A Tale of Two Universes: The Mythology of Play

This world is not a theater, in which we can laugh; and we are not assembled together in order to burst into peals of laughter, but to weep for our sins. But some of you still want to say: "I would prefer God to give me the chance to go on laughing and joking." Is there anything more childish than thinking in this way? It is not God who gives us the chance to play, but the devil.[1]

—SAINT CHRYSOSTOM

The highest Lord, due to his fullness, plays spontaneously by imitating the ways of the separate beings, having become each of them due to his reeling under the intoxication of bliss.[2]

—UTPALADEVA

THE DAY SHE DESTROYED THE UNIVERSE

No one will let her forget the day she destroyed the universe.

Some would even consider it more noteworthy than the separation of day from night and the breathing of sentient life into matter.

The hands of time will never move quite as slowly as when you reach out into the unknown, tentatively, but rapturously, yearning for contact with the object of your desire. The one you are not supposed to touch. The one that would clearly precipitate your downfall, while also, just maybe, revealing a new world.

Under the glaring disapproval of the newborn sun, she looked up at that apple, suspended in what felt like eternity. Her whole body quivered, and she felt a flush of heat below, in a place she'd never felt before. Then she reached a little farther, touched its smooth skin, pulled it off the branch, and took a bite.

The rest, as they say, is history. In fact, we are to believe that history as we know it did not begin until this moment—the moment that First Woman made contact with First Desire, felt it in her body and, determining that it was good, said yes. The immediate consequences of this decision included, among other things, the subordination of woman to man; the cursing of the Earth; and the cosmic arrival of death itself.

Yeesh.

I KNOW IT MAY SEEM STRANGE to begin a discussion of play with a retelling of Biblical mythology, but play can hardly be understood in this culture without reference to its primary impediment. Consciously and unconsciously, our culture has been shaped in relation to this origin myth and the various beliefs it necessitates we hold to support its veracity.

For the myths we live by create our experience of reality. They shape our attitudes toward the world and ourselves by illustrating patterns of behavior to be rewarded or punished, delineating our ideas of good and bad in the process. This myth places us squarely in Eden's shadow, tossed outside her boundaries with no purpose to fulfill, only earnest and solemn penitence, praying that redemption may be bestowed upon us so that we may rejoin the holy play. Again and again, our dour commitment to this narrative reifies the joylessness it proclaims we deserve, leaving us powerless to deviate from the ordained script.

Forgetting that there is a myth involved, we come to mistake the map for the territory, the myth for the universe itself. And we as a culture have so absorbed the Fall from Eden mythology that, even in this secular age, we unknowingly treat its implications as fundamental to the universe.

The whole of our society—its institutions, economic systems, patterns of relationship, interpretations of gender, nature, order, chaos, ethics, values, and morals—proceeds from this myth. And the primary assumption, the one underlying and generating all the others, is that to correctly live this life is to rid oneself of the playful and innocent desire that led Eve into this whole mess to begin with.

But there is good news. The very act of recognizing that this grim universe is not the universe *as such,* but rather the universe filtered through a particular myth, opens degrees of freedom where previously there was only fatalism, levity where there was oppressive heaviness. For at other times, and in other places, cultures other than our own have lived with other myths that led them to place playfulness and fulfillment high on their priorities. From the divine child's play of Homeric Greece's Hermes to the playful inversions of the Native American trickster Coyote, to the erotic dalliances of the Hindu play-god Krishna, the playful approach to life is not just a speculative hypothesis: It has been rigorously tested and explored by a variety of cultures and codified as myths that have endured across the centuries.

These cultures have found out that the more we see life as inherently playful, the more fulfilled and creative we're going to be. Because play increases empathy and cooperation, reduces violence, neutralizes tension with levity and humor, and facilitates novel approaches to problem-solving. As numerous studies have shown, play helps us learn and retain knowledge, shapes our brain, and lends us the flexibility to adapt to a changing world.

Play also lets us dream up new realities in which to reconsider the meanings and possibilities of our lives. The irony is that the play-denying Eden myth was dreamed up in just such a way: Through the free play

3

of the creative imagination, an otherworldly garden, a rogue serpent, an unbridled woman, and a primal man were conjured into existence. The drama that unfolded between them, as well as the social and psychological implications of that drama, were similarly dreamed into existence, blooming from the fertile minds of inspired mythmakers in ancient Near Eastern religious communities and in the theological writings of the early Christian monastics and doctrinarians that elaborated upon those myths.

By examining the myth of Eden, we can discern and so untie ourselves from the imaginal threads by which these desert fathers have bound us to their asceticism. For with discernment comes choice, and with choice comes freedom—in this case, the freedom to enter an otherwise unknowable reality.

To provide a template of this other reality—and because play is most fun when the players are well-matched—we will contrast the seriousness of Eden with the playfulness that Hindus refer to as *Lila* (Sanskrit for "Divine Play"). The myths that arise to demonstrate Lila's role in creation first emerged in a collection of religious texts, beginning in the fourth century—right around the time that early Christian theologians were putting the finishing touches on their more dour worldview. And Lila presents a radically different framework through which to interpret our experience.

A few hundred years of consequence later, we can investigate how these differing worldviews have influenced the world around us and our perception of it. We can use the Eden myth as an exemplar of a broader myth of seriousness, and the Lila myth as an exemplar of a broader myth of play, to ask ourselves questions like: What specifically are the implications of the serious myth? And what are the implications of the play myth? How do they compare? And, if life were really meant to be played ecstatically rather than struggled against seriously, what would change?

The point here is not to promote some exotic Eastern spirituality over our more familiar Western traditions. Instead, our intention is to use the features of a more playful myth to make explicit the implicit seriousness we've absorbed as a civilization; to contrast that seriousness with the possibility of play; and to see what shifts arise in our assumptions, expectations, and perceptions of reality in the process.

To that end, we will pull apart the cultural, historical, and philosophical roots of the Eden myth, to determine how we ended up in a world where enjoyment itself is treated with suspicion, if not outright derision. For our serious worldview did not just fall out of the sky, as a divine edict (although its proponents may tell you otherwise). On the contrary, it was consciously worked out by a handful of theologians who set the foundations, and thus dictated the direction, of our civilization.

We are thankfully blessed with the same arbitrary license with which they dreamed their serious world into being, and by our own free choice may dream a more playful world into being, to remember the innate playfulness that the filter of seriousness has concealed from us.

SERPENT WISDOM

Let's begin with an evaluation of the Eden myth, the elements and outcomes of this serious-minded perspective. It asserts our origin in clear terms and consequences, the experience of our entire life and all those before us and after determined by an infraction committed on an entirely separate playing field: a garden governed by a single, arbitrary rule.

If we are to take this myth and its moral as true, we consequentially take on a slew of resulting beliefs, which impact on our perception of ourselves and the world we inhabit. First, we would come to believe ourselves to be of a universe in which curiosity, desire, exploration of the unknown, creative engagement with the environment, and playing with the rules will cast us into disaster. The moment that Eve said yes to that serpent, she triggered the calamity that comes when an unattended woman is moved by her impulse, motivated by her desire, taken by her own rapture.

The connection between the serpent's wisdom and feminine desire was deliberate and quite the coup for the side of seriousness. The civilizations that surrounded the authors of this myth had, for thousands of years, been worshiping a goddess whom they consistently depicted either as or in relation to a serpent. To take just a few examples: Nidaba, the neighboring Sumerian goddess and patron deity of writing, was often depicted as a serpent; the nearby Elamite religion had a deep reverence for serpent magic, which it saw as an aspect of the archetypal feminine; and the Babylonian Ishtar, seated on her heavenly throne, held a staff encircled by serpents. As Merlin Stone writes in *When God Was a Woman*: "It can hardly have been chance or coincidence that it was a serpent who offered Eve the advice. For people of that time knew that the serpent was the symbol, perhaps even the instrument, of divine counsel in the religion of the Goddess."

By casting the serpent as the antagonist of their drama, the authors of the Eden myth implied that not only woman but the feminine nature intrinsic to the human psyche—which expresses itself as primal hunger and rapturous desire—is by its very existence a kind of subversion or disobedience of the Lord of the universe. These impulses are fundamental to our nature, but by the centuries of persuasion, we have come to see our nature itself as inherently suspect. The message becomes clear: Who we are and what we feel in the moment should be suppressed, or at least minimized, to avoid incurring wrath. But this, of course, assumes we live in a wrathful universe characterized by divine punishment. A universe that compels fear. A universe in which life must be endured, as the laws of our nature are contrary to the laws of divinity.

The God of Eden, then, is a kind of cosmic librarian, forever shushing the humor out of our experience, shaming us into an earnest solemnity. He demands that we be suspicious of our hunger, our desire, our exploratory impulse, and our creative impulse—in a word, our play impulse. To enter an exploratory relationship with the unknown elements of the environment, to taste the apple, is to risk going off the rails of a preordained life; encountering something novel and integrating it into our being; taking in the unknown as though it were a sacrament. And to do so would be to risk overstepping our place as *created* and not *creator*. To play with the rules, to go out of bounds, is to repeat the primordial pattern that resulted in our descent into this punitive world in the first place. Not advisable.

The next implication of this myth is that this world is not our home, but rather a prison into which we have been confined for our first parents' sins. According to Genesis 3:17–18, in the words of the God of Eden: "On your account the earth will be cursed. You will get your food from it only by labor all the days of your life; it will yield thorns and thistles for you." I seriously doubt this God considered that some of us might actually be aroused by the occasional thorn or thistle, or that even the prickliest sensation might hold the potential for pleasure. His intention, rather, was to speak into creation a one-sided and one-dimensional universe, where pain is pain, pleasure is pleasure, and categories are definitive, not to be mixed.

It follows that to take pleasure in this world is to miss the point of this world. To let yourself be carried away by the same gentle rapture that bends the blades of grass, to be delightfully saturated by the warmth of the sun, to dance with the leaves as they whirl in the autumn wind, would be to find pleasure in a world made for suffering. And to risk a personal sense of enjoyment by finding a loophole in a world made for suffering would mean risking more wrath: Another fall, another punishment from this world of suffering into a hell-world of more suffering. And if the thought of an afterlife of agonizing bondage sounds at all alluring to us, we had better not let our Lord and Master know it.

The devout would have us believe that our predicament was gravely serious for the reason that they remained single-mindedly focused on their solitary objective. They played without taking enjoyment in the pursuit and would encourage us to endure our suffering with equal stoicism, restraining any impulse to transform it to delight. As St. Ambrose put it in his *De Officiis*: "Joking should be avoided even in small talk, so that some more serious topic is not made light of. 'Woe unto you who laugh now; you shall mourn and weep,' (Luke 6:25) saith the Lord: are we then looking for something to laugh at, so that we may laugh now but weep hereafter?"

Although the writings of church fathers like Saint Ambrose may seem antiquated and therefore irrelevant, their theology laid much of the philosophical groundwork for our Western civilization and its implicit assumptions. These men took the raw material of mythology and scripture and crystallized it into doctrine—into a codified framework through which to view and relate to reality. And, according to them, anything ecstatic or joyous—such as laughter, arousal, playfulness, or spontaneous dance—is meant to be restrained.

Saint John Chrysostom, one of the most prolific writers of early Christian commentary continued this humorless bend in one of his more famous sermons: "This world is not a theatre, in which we can laugh; and we are not assembled together in order to burst into peals of laughter, but to weep for our sins. But some of you still want to say: 'I would prefer God to give me the chance to go on laughing and joking.' Is there anything more childish than thinking in this way? It is not God who gives us the chance to play, but the devil."[3]

In fact, according to Saint Gregory of Nyssa, another early church father, the termination of the cosmic dance itself was a direct consequence of Eve's sin:

> Once there was a time when the whole of rational creation formed a single dancing chorus looking upward to the one leader of this dance . . . but the beginning of sin made an end of the sweet sounds of this chorus . . . since then man . . . must sweat and most arduously toil to do battle with and conquer the spirit that, thanks to sin, now weighs upon him; but the spoils of victory will be these . . . once again he will take part in the dancing of the divine chorus. . . . be sure that . . . thou art being warned not to succumb in the battle against temptation but to look steadfastly forward to the final victory. And this victory shall come and thou shalt be found in the dancing ranks of the angelic spirits.[4]

AN IMPERFECT WORLD

For as dusty and uncomfortable as we may imagine old Saint Gregory to have been, earnestly writing out his biblical commentaries in fourth-century Turkey, we can be grateful he at least maintained hope to one day be invited to dance again. But it's specifically the stark contrast between the world in which he imagines we must "arduously toil to do battle with," striving to achieve "the final victory . . . in the dancing ranks of the angelic spirits" that points to the next implication the Eden myth would foist upon us.

This overarching doctrine is that we live in a world of teleology, with somewhere to get to and no time to enjoy the journey. The etymology of the word comes from the Greek *telos,* meaning "end, goal, result," and *logia,* meaning "doctrine, theory, science." Teleology, then, is the doctrine of the goal, the theory of the end result, the science of reducing everything in life to a distant aim. To dance now, in this world, then, is to succumb to temptation, to violate the cosmic order, and to therefore be deprived of the opportunity to dance in the eternal hereafter. Conversely, to toil and "do battle" against dancing in this world is to be granted the opportunity to dance one day in heaven.

The trouble is, it's not possible to be in two places at once: We are either in the here and now, which is real, or the there and then, which is imagined. So, to relate to life teleologically is to allow it to pass by without being present in it.

There is nothing wrong with having goals in life. But the more we remove ourselves from the present moment, devaluing the immediacy of experience with the expectation that one day things will be better than they are now, the less present we are to the beauty of life as it already is.

To strive toward the perfection of an end goal is to render the present universe imperfect, to treat life as inadequate, and so harbor a kind of contempt. An antagonistic dynamic arises, in which the present is seen as the enemy of the future. But, because we are ourselves inseparable from the present world—inhaling its oxygen into our lungs, taking its moisture into our cells, feeling its warmth on our skin—then we must also hold ourselves in contempt, must see ourselves as the enemy. We hate ourselves now so as to love ourselves later.

This is, of course, a losing game. But we don't see it, especially since we have blinded ourselves to any real sense of play. Instead, we treat the "hate now, love later" game as the seriousness of life itself. In Timothy 4:10, Saint Paul says: "For to this end we toil and strive, because we have our hope set on the living God, who is the savior of all people." By this he means: To live in the serious world is to toil and strive for an end—the end of our life in this world, and the beginning of our life in another, hoped-for world. To enjoy this world, then, is to not toil and strive and, by implication, not be saved.

If we assume that the purpose of our lives is to get somewhere in the future, at the expense of our creative engagement with the present, then spontaneity, surprise, and unpredictability occur as violations. These unwanted interruptions of our plans threaten to draw us into the devalued present and derail us from our steadfast fixation on the future.

If life is only a means to an end, then living becomes an exercise in controlling, limiting, and staving off unpredictability, restraining spontaneity, suppressing surprise. Unable to let go, we brace against our experience in the fear that it may inconvenience us. We take the same route to work every day, because it's the most efficient, forgoing the slightly longer but significantly more beautiful scenic route through the mountains. We have things delivered to our doorstep by anonymous postal workers rather than venturing out into the funky old store down the street. We order the same meal at the same restaurant every time we go, even though we've been going there for five years now. Our lives become smaller and smaller, excluding more of nature and more of humanity, reducing the dynamism of lived and felt experience to the static linearity of anticipated outcome. Life itself becomes something we must avoid, paradoxically, to perpetuate life—in some distant, hoped-for future. We sacrifice a lived life for a promised life and enter a pattern of behavior intended to secure that promise.

As a result, when in the teleological universe, we shape our lives around our fear of disapproval and our craving for acknowledgment. This makes us controllable by outside forces, whether human or divine, which may, at any moment, withdraw the security of their love. But this myth isn't the only way of viewing and relating to reality. Although its implications are familiar, they are not necessary. At other times, and in other places, people have lived according to other myths, with other principles, and other implicit assumptions.

To explore what it might be like to live outside the boundaries and consequences of the Eden myth, let's now turn to the perspective of Lila, the myth of divine play. The Sanskrit word *Lila* translates into both the verb and noun forms of the English word *play*, pointing to both the action and the world it conjures. Elements of this mythology occur in a collection of Hindu religious texts, such as the Harivamsa and the Bhagavata, Vishnu, and Brahmavaivarta Puranas. Krishna appears throughout each of these texts, acting out his playful shenanigans in his myriad forms—the divine child, the holy prankster, the erotic reveler. In these stories, he serves as a personification of playfulness, the creative force from which our world has emerged and through which it continually reorganizes itself.

There are two major metaphors used to demonstrate Lila: that the universe is a dance, and that the universe is a game of hide-and-seek.

SANDCASTLES BY THE SEA

As opposed to the elements of temptation and transgression in the Eden myth that precipitate our circumstance, the foundation of Lila assumes that the universe was ecstatically danced into being as an act of divine play. In this mythology, the Lord of the universe, as "Lord of the Dance," ecstatically whirls the world into creation only to eventually dance it into dissolution. Like a child who builds a sandcastle by the seashore and then stands to watch it wash away in the tide, the divinity conjures our world into being, simply because it's more fun than not doing so, and with as much joy remains unattached as it dissolves, knowing he can, and likely will, simply regenerate it instantaneously.

Hinduism perceives the functions of the universe in three ways, each personified by a particular divinity, collectively known as the Trimurti.

Brahma is Lord of Creation, Vishnu is Lord of Preservation, and Shiva is Lord of Destruction, though we should not project our Western fear of death to his role, carried out with as much divine reverence as the other two functions. Before the creation of the universe, the infinite and eternal being Vishnu exists reclining on the cosmic serpent Ananta. In his dream, a vision of creation arises, sprouting a lotus from his navel, marking the beginning of the cosmic cycle. Brahma emerges from this lotus, symbolizing the birth of the universe from the infinite. He separates the flower into Earth, sky, and heavens, and then divides his own brilliant body into male and female forms, an expression of the nature that gave rise to himself.[5]

Vishnu, for his part, incarnates within creation, enacting his divine play to preserve its manifestation. The most beloved of these incarnations is of course Krishna who repeatedly and joyously immerses himself in the dance of this world. In one story, the deity Krishna, on a moonlit night, is overcome by the beauty of this world and begins to play a song on his flute. The song is so spellbinding that the local maidens all run off to meet him, leaving behind their husbands, their children, their livestock, and their duties, even as family members try to block their way. Meeting them in an open field, Krishna transforms himself into sixteen thousand forms, so as to appear to each woman as the face of her desire. Satisfying their yearning to be his partner and his lover, he dances and frolics with them late into the evening:

Embracing them with wandering arms;
playfully touching their hands
with the tips of his fingernails
Which then fell upon their breasts,
belts, thighs, and hair;
Conversing coyly

with glances and laughter,
He joyfully awakened the god of love
in those beautiful young women . . . [6]

In this myth, not only is the universe danced into existence, but the most exalted form of worship is to dance back, to participate in and savor the cosmic dance of the divinity—playfully and flirtatiously, with glances and laughter.

To view the world as play, then, is to treat it less like a trip with a set destination and more like a partner calling out for you to dance. We don't dance from a place of burden and irritation, hoping to get the thing over with as soon as possible. Rather, we dance to surrender to the rhythm, to experience harmony with the music and with our partner. We dance to be taken delightfully out of control.

The same is true for music. Musicians don't play in order to finish their song as soon as they can. They play for a sense of creative flow, for a mystical participation that is immediate, rapturous, spellbinding, and complete. To truly dance, to truly make music, is to step into infinity as a cocreator. It is to melt away the finitude of the identity such that the infinite can be heard, felt, shared, and known.

In this rapturous participation, the dancer is a Sufi dervish, whirling themselves into God, joining the cosmic dance. Along with the divinity, who creates and consumes everything in the dancing flames of their ecstatic joy, the dancer scatters their identity like ashes into the sea and delightfully dissolves into the movement of the waves.

A PLAYFUL UNIVERSE IS AUTOTELIC

Because play can only take place in the present moment, a playful universe is an autotelic universe, with nowhere to get to and timeless enjoyment to be had. The etymology, in this case, comes from *auto,* meaning "self," and *telic,* again meaning "end." In contrast to a teleological approach to life, which treats experiences as stepping-stones toward an end, the autotelic approach treats present experience as the end in itself: every step of the dance is a new beginning, and every note in the song is the purpose of playing.

To live an autotelic life is to live from a state of rapt absorption in the flow of experience, dissolving into the stream of life such that the boundaries between self and environment begin to merge. Like Jimi Hendrix setting his guitar on fire and dancing along with its flames; like Biggie Smalls freestyling on a Brooklyn street corner, anchoring the weight of his body into the pavement as the electric power of his poetry flows through him. Like the Zen calligrapher whose brush unites body, mind, ink, and rice paper, penetrating their being just as the ink saturates the page. These are the players of an autotelic life.

As they are already being rewarded in the here and now, the autotelic person has no concern for future rewards—whatever angelic choirs may or may not be waiting down the road have no bearing on the fun available in this moment's dance. That is not to say that these players are averse to challenges that might even overtake them, far from it— their nature roots them into the depths of play such that they are willing to risk everything in the moment. Like the hang glider who soars off the edge of a cliff, risking their life in the process, the autotelic person throws themselves wholeheartedly into the play of existence for no goal other than to continue playing. Paradoxically, by releasing any attempts to control the future, the autotelic person arrives at a future worth having, along with the capacity to savor and enjoy it.

Rather than trying to avoid failure at all costs lest their perfection be tarnished and their place in heaven revoked, the autotelic person expands the arena of play wide enough to include and even relish failures. It is precisely what survives from game to game, each outcome simply a manifestation arising and turning back to the sea. In fact, as play researcher Nicole Lazzaro has found, game players "spend nearly all of their time failing. Roughly four times out of five, gamers don't complete the mission, run out of time, don't solve the puzzle, lose the fight, fail to improve their score, crash and burn, or [in the case of a video game] die."[7] But, unlike in non-playful contexts, these failures do not discourage the players. Instead of eliciting feelings of shame, despair, or self-judgment, they inspire deeper engagement with the game.

The mechanism underlying these startling findings was discovered by the M.I.N.D Labs (Media Interface and Network Design Labs) in Helsinki, Finland, which measured players' heart rate and skin conductivity, as well as the electrical activation of their facial muscles, while playing a video game, an efficient form of play to measure in a controlled setting. The researchers determined that players displayed "the most potent combination of positive emotions when they made a mistake."[8]

This was by design: Every time the players made a mistake in the game, a monkey on the screen would immediately be sent flying off into outer space. In addition to making them laugh, this reinforced the players' sense of agency in the game: Even when they failed, something remarkable and amusing happened.

When we pay attention to our lives, without attachment to outcome, something remarkable and amusing happens in even our most stupendous failures. In these instances, we find the levity and courage to smile and play in even those moments that trigger our fears or damage our pride—like an unexpected illness, a messy divorce, or a business going bankrupt—we recover a sense of agency over our lives. In the case of the video game players, this positive association with failure very quickly created a feedback loop, which sparked feelings of "excitement, joy, and interest" in the players and invigorated their desire to play, no matter what.[9]

16

This orientation toward the world is what naturally arises from an outlook based on playful mythology: If the universe is play, and the play is occurring just as much now as it will later, then there's nowhere to get to and nothing to be afraid of. You're already there. Meeting the cosmic dance as it naturally unfolds, we allow ourselves to be surprised at every turn. We have no plans to be undermined, and even if we do, we delight in the opportunity to surrender to a deeper plan: the unfolding plan of nature, the cosmic dance of the divine. With each disruption of our ego's plans, an opening appears, a crack in the façade, an interval, a space through which our essential nature can reveal itself.

INTERPLAY OF OPPOSITES

Just as you could not have sound without silence and movement without stillness, the great dance of life proceeds by an interplay of opposites. A tornado cannot take form without the space between its particles of dust and rain. Even the densest stones vibrate imperceptibly, and between their densely packed atoms, space swims, pushing back against the oppressive solidity and finitude.

Consider the role of silence in music: How it is the tension of emptiness that lends potency and gravity to the punctuating beat; the longing for contact that electrifies a symphony; the torture of inevitability that grieves a song into being. The vulnerability of knowing that nonbeing is insolubly bound to being and choosing to play anyway, to write anyway, to dance anyway—joining the great sweeping tide of universes arising and dissolving, emerging and disintegrating—requires a courage that is itself a hallmark of divinity. Needing nothing, the god clings not to the forms of this world. Needing nothing, players in touch with their inward divinity let go and allow themselves to be carried by grace. Like the sandcastle built on the shore of the ocean, life is built only to be washed away, along with the entirety of the universe. But rather than treat this as a cause for despair, the play spirit takes this finitude as a constraint through which to access the infinite on an even more intimate level. Suddenly, death itself, along with everything else, becomes part of the game.

And though the dissolutive chaos encircles the rapture always, engulfing the lustrous flashes of radiant light with rings of darkness, nevertheless the ecstasy of being continues, outpacing nonbeing by a slender enough margin to keep the game interesting. To put it in the words of the *Bhagavata Purana,* one of the primary sources of Lila mythology: Although they were surrounded "by a ring of dark clouds," the lovers of the divine play of life. . . .

While dancing,
. . . sang out loud
and the throats of those
so delighted by love
became reddened.
They were overjoyed
by the touch of Krishna,
and the whole universe
became filled
with their song.

One of them . . .
sang out in pure embellished tones,
freely improvising on a melody.
Pleased by her performance,
he honored her, saying
"Well done!" "Well done!"
Another one sang out that melody

in a stylized rhythmic pattern,
and he offered her much praise.

Then one of them placed
on her shoulder
the arm of Krishna,
with the fragrance
of a blue lotus.
Upon smelling this scent,
blended with the balm
of sandalwood,
she became elated
with bodily ripplings of bliss
and kissed his arm tenderly.

Thus with his hands
touching them in embraces,
With broad playful smiles
and affectionate glances,
The Lord of Rama delighted in
loving the fair maidens . . .
Just as a small child plays
with his own reflection.[10]

THE UNIVERSE AS HIDE AND SEEK

This comparison between the "fair maidens" and "his own reflection" illustrates how the play myth conceptualizes the relation between world and divinity. In this myth, God—out of sheer curiosity and play, wanting more than anything to explore every facet of existence—has hidden himself in every part of the universe. As the ninth-century mystic and philosopher of Lila, Somananda put it, "Just as a king over the whole earth, in the joyous and startled intoxication of his sovereignty, can play at being a simple soldier, imitating his behavior, so in His beatitude the Lord amuses himself by assuming the multiple forms of the earth."[11]

In this great cosmic game of hide-and-seek, God scatters himself in every part of existence, and not only hides himself, but also forgets that he has been hidden, and forgets even that he is God. From there, the game begins: The hidden God in each of us begins to seek his or her own reflection in every other part of the universe, to play with it, wanting nothing more than to be discovered and seen through the eyes of another, intimately, vulnerably, and honestly.

In contrast to the Fall from Eden myth, where God stands above and outside the world as a punitive judge, here God descends into the world of manifold experience—and not only the pleasant parts. One scripture even says that "as a game, [God] takes on the form of the bodies abiding in the gulf of the oceans of hell."[12]

Here, the addict, the prostitute, the sick person, the bereaved, and even the hopeless are all manifestations of a god who wants to play in all dimensions of life. Freely and wholeheartedly, he enters a torture chamber in Guantanamo Bay, a crack house in New Orleans's Ninth Ward, a leper colony in Mumbai, and a child-soldier training camp in the Congolese jungle. But whereas the Eden myth would treat these painful experiences as God's will, the Lila myth refers instead to them as God's play. They are not realms of punishment but realms of complex, dynamic experience, dramatic scenes in the play of life, their inhabitants as equal in their divine potential as the priestess or conqueror—to acknowledge them as anything less would be to limit them with our own pity and judgment.

The playful orientation to life offered through Lila treats every experience as if it were a theatrical scene—a dramatic movement, a potent performance. And in the unfolding narrative of this cosmic drama, God wants nothing less than to get lost, to stray, to wander, to know distance from himself, to experience the total forgetting of his own divinity.

God confines himself to the constraints of a finite life and forgets that he has chosen it—only to see if he can spot the reflection of his own divinity and remember who he really is along the way. In this view, the unhappily married woman looking to satiate her hunger in a shame-drenched affair, as well as the homeless junkie on the streets begging for enough change to secure his next hit are manifestations of the hidden god who has forgotten his own divinity. And this forgetfulness is not an accident or a condition to be overcome; it is the means by which the god of play comes to know every facet of his creation from the inside out.

Consider that you are a god, and that, after millions of lifetimes spent inhabiting the consciousness of mystics, healers, lovers, and artists, you have grown slightly bored. *I wonder what's going on in the other side of town*, you think, and decide to descend into the darkness: to know the concrete isolation of a solitary cell or the splintered delirium of the schizophrenic's madness. Consider that you have conjured up this very life that you are living now, out of sheer curiosity for what it might be like to be you—to experience your uniquely unsavory set of circumstances, in your moment of history, in your corner of the world. And only by forgetting your divinity could you inhabit the fullness of this particular life wholeheartedly.

In fact—and for this reason—in some cases this forgetfulness is rated even higher than the remembrance of divinity. In one of the Lila tales, the young Krishna's friends tell his mother, Yasoda, that he has been out eating clay. And when she asks him if their accusations are true, he insists that they are lying and even implores her to check in his mouth for proof. And when she opens his mouth:

> There, within that tiny aperture, Yasoda beholds all moving and nonmoving entities, outer space, and all directions, along with mountains, islands, oceans, the surface of the earth, the planetary systems, the moon, the stars, the wind, fire, air, sky and creation . . . Finally, in the midst of it all, she sees herself. . . . Struck with wonder, Yasoda begins to question whether she is witnessing a dream . . . or, in fact, some inherent divine power of her dearmost son. In a mood of deep veneration, she begins to offer homage to Him who is beyond the conception of human speculation. . . . Understanding his mother's absorption in high philosophical contemplation, the omnipotent supreme master . . . inspires her to once again become immersed in intense maternal affection for him. Immediately, all such contemplations fly from Yasoda's memory. With a heart overflowing with intense love, she takes Krishna on her lap as before, returning to the previous state of mind.[13]

Here, reality and illusion, the sacred and the profane, are intermixed and subsumed in divine play, which could not proceed without both aspects of existence. This illusion of mortality, this forgetfulness of divinity, only serves to increase the humor, the drama, and the fun of the game. In one Lila tale, for example, the infant god Krishna forgets his own divinity, just so he can give away all his mom's yogurt to the local monkeys. And when she catches him in the act, he runs away screaming and crying, trying anxiously to escape her punishment. Rather than lording it over the universe, that is, this god decides it would be more fun to play the part of an unruly toddler, trying his best to outrun his mommy! By freely exchanging his power, handing it over to his mortal mother or his human devotees, the god Krishna increases the range of his play. With each reversal of the cosmic order, with each inversion of the rules, something new is revealed.

PLAYING WITH BOUNDARIES

As opposed to the Western Lord of covenant and judgment, the god of play wants to know what it's like to break the rules, to move beyond the ordered boundaries of priestly and cultural codes to experience their shadow, their opposite. In another Lila tale, Krishna repeatedly refuses and thwarts his mother's every attempt to feed him. But when she tells him not to steal the household butter while she's away, he criminally devours the entire jar. When she comes home and spots him next to the empty jar with a face covered in butter, she reprimands him for breaking her one and only rule.

To this he replies wryly, "But mother, how could I have stolen the butter? Doesn't everything in the house belong to us?[14]

And she laughs! Here, in total contrast to the Eden myth, it is the god himself who eats the forbidden food, the god himself who refuses the abundance (here, of his mother's cooking; there, of the garden's bounty), in order to consume precisely the food that is out of bounds. And when he is caught, rather than hide in shame, he makes a joke.

By surrendering to his inner impulse instead of external codes, Krishna exemplifies the total freedom of the creative spirit, which moves autotelically from its own inspiration, keeping all doors open. To act from impulse rather than rules requires a deep connection to the self, the body, the spirit—to an inward law with its own dictates. This devotion to the spirit revitalizes the foundations of a world that, absent periodic disruption, would calcify into empty legalism, robbing life of everything that makes it worth living. As the mythologist Lewis Hyde puts it, "As the thief of butter Krishna upsets the categories that his mother has established to separate him . . . because the abundance that Krishna wants (or represents) is available only when the structure has been removed . . . prepared foods are sustenance filtered through a net of cultural conditions. Stolen butter, on the other hand, is unconditioned, immediate, concentrated."[15]

The play world, then, is a world in which reality—its limits, categories, and constraints—is ever up for reinterpretation. In this world, boundaries are meant to be played with, rather than played within. Unlike the Eden myth, in which the transgression of boundaries warrants divine wrath, in the play world of Lila, boundary violations are the necessary starting points for the continuation of the game. Because a world of static boundaries tends to grow rigid and stale, playing with these limits is a life-giving act. The alternative to this playfulness is a slow decline into dysfunction and decay. As play researcher Stuart Brown, founder of the National Institute for Play, puts it, "When we stop playing, we stop developing, and when that happens, the laws of entropy take over—things fall apart. Ultimately, we . . . become vegetative, staying in one spot, not fully interacting with the world, more plant than animal. When we stop playing, we start dying."[16]

WHICH WILL YOU CHOOSE?

We have a choice, then, between two universes: A serious universe, in which curiosity, desire, exploration of the unknown, creative engagement with the environment, and (most of all) playing with the rules leads to disaster. A world of teleology, with somewhere to get to and no time to enjoy the journey. A world of heaviness, authority, and hierarchy, in which meaning is fixed, power is oppressive, and humor is suspect. A world of divine wrath, where the universe compels fear, and life must be endured. A world of barely controlled unpredictability that occurs as violation. A mechanical, deterministic world of survival. A finite world of primal guilt.

Or—and it is such a subtle shift in perception—a playful universe in which curiosity, desire, exploration of the unknown, and creative engagement with the environment are seen as sacred. A world where boundaries are meant to be played with. An autotelic world, with nowhere to go, and timeless enjoyment to be had. A world of levity, humor, inversions, and loopholes. A world in which meaning is fluid and power is freely exchanged. A world in which reality itself—its limits, categories, and constraints—is up for reinterpretation. A world of spontaneity, surprise, involuntary rapture, and surrender. A cosmic world of dancing, rhythm, harmony, and (most important) fun. An infinite, open-ended, and organic world of living, connected beings experiencing primal joy and vulnerability.

This is an invitation to consider that second universe available just beyond the walls constructed by the Eden myth and its consequential beliefs, the option beckoning from the periphery of our narrowed, finite awareness. For what you now see as failure, you may come to see as freedom. What you now see as suffering, you may alchemize into ecstasy. What you now see as an obstacle, you may come to see as a call to mastery. To put it in the words of one of history's finest players, Marcus Aurelius, you may find that "the impediment to action advances action. What stands in the way becomes the way."

We invite you to play.

2

The Elements of Play

Play cannot be defined, because in play all definitions slither, dance, combine, break apart, and recombine.[1]

—STEPHEN NACHMANOVITCH

In short, it seems the problems in characterizing play are indeed insolvable. Other pitfalls await.[2]

—GORDON BURGHARDT

FINDING PLAY

The biologist E. O. Wilson writes that "no behavioral concept has proven more ill-defined, elusive, controversial, and even unfashionable than play."[3] On the one hand, we all know it when we see it: the wagging tail on a golden retriever, the delightfully messy toddler's finger painting, the street kid kicking an old soccer ball between two trash cans in a Rio favela. But when it comes to defining exactly what play is, things get a little trickier. Definitions derive power from their lines of demarcation, from the clarity of their categories. But play, by its very nature, is squiggly, wily, and impossible to pin down. It arises from a dimension of our being that is preverbal—more ancient than language, more primal than symbolic thought—and manages to play with words without being bound by them.

We could call it a biological impulse, and we would not be wrong. Animals spontaneously engage in play behavior, facilitating trust and complex social organization in the process. Play-fighting bears, for example, establish through their pawing, nipping, and wrestling that neither of them will kill or seriously injure the other; that they can experiment, take risks, stretch their range, and experience a greater freedom of movement. Play allows animals to discover who they are, what they're capable of, and how they can creatively engage with their surroundings. It helps them stay flexible, responsive, and attuned to real-time changes in their physical and social environments. And, at least in the case of humans, play provides us with the freedom to reformulate our image of the world in response to these changes.

Play even fosters brain development along the way. To reference just one of many studies, the animal play researcher John Byers found that the amount of play affects the development of the brain's frontal cortex, the brain region responsible for much cognition—discriminating relevant material from irrelevant, planning, and organizing our thoughts and feelings.[4]

Yet a reduction to biology and its motivations feels unsatisfying. There is something ineffable about play. This irreducible element, the spirit of play, provides us with the inner freedom and security needed to venture beyond the physical and the known and discover that our hard-wired biological limits are in fact malleable. We could therefore call play the spirit through which life expands to arrange itself in ever-increasing complexity; the self-transcendent impulse; the invisible power that moves us to forget our finitude and remember our divinity.

But, where the biological definition feels too concrete and pragmatic, this spiritual definition feels too ungrounded and imprecise. We are therefore left with the question: how do we include the inner experience of play, with all its psychic and spiritual potency, without leaving behind play's connection to nature—to the physical body, our evolutionary history, and the sensuality of our surroundings?

PLAYING WITH WORDS

The classic definition of play comes from the Dutch historian Johan Huizinga, who writes that play is "a free activity standing quite consciously outside 'ordinary' life as being 'not serious' but at the same time absorbing the player intensely and utterly. It is an activity connected with no material interest, and no profit can be gained from it. It proceeds within its own boundaries of time and space according to fixed rules and in an orderly manner. . . ."[5]

Implicit in Huizinga's definition is the understanding that play is play simply because it says so. The moment that two or more players freely come together and decide to mark off their activity as play, whatever takes place in that magic circle is "not serious," regardless of its content. The firmest spank, which may otherwise have been a source of grief or trauma, can instead become a source of ecstasy and delight, simply by virtue of being predetermined as playful.

Yet Huizinga's definition still feels too narrow. First of all, he assumes that all play must proceed within set boundaries of time and space, have fixed rules, and be orderly. But what about the kind of play—like Krishna stealing his mother's yogurt and giving it away to the local monkeys—that plays with boundaries, treats rules as malleable, and relishes disorderly behavior? Huizinga also assumes that play is a kind of activity. But, as illustrated by the example of consensual spanking, it may be more precise to call play the spirit with which an activity is done, rather than the activity itself. Put another way, play is a matter of context rather than content, of orientation to activity rather than substance of activity.

So, our initial quandary remains: How do we define something that, by its very nature, disrupts the fixed categories that definitions rely upon?

One option would be to play with the word itself: to pick it apart and play with its pieces. We could turn it over, like kids overturning old stones in the woods. We could dig into its roots, like retrievers digging up old bones. We could dance with its various turns of meaning, walking together with them along winding, uncertain paths, teasing out a picture from many angles, or at least cultivating a relationship, some intimacy, along the way.

ON LOVE AND SORCERY

Our modern English word "play" comes from the Old English *plegan,* meaning "to move lightly and quickly."[6] It is connected to the Middle Dutch *pleyen,* "to dance,"[7] as well as a cluster of other Germanic words that all trace back to a common Indo-European root, originally meaning "to vouch or stand guard for, to take a risk, to expose oneself to danger for someone or something."[8] A *plegan* was a sacred act, an oath, through which you would "bind or engage" your spirit entirely to your action.[9] From this we derive our modern English words "pledge"[10] and "plight."[11] Along these lines, in some Germanic languages, "you can *'pflegen'* homage, thanks . . . mourning, work, love," and even "sorcery."[12]

To play, in its original meaning, then, is to expose your vulnerability, to put your life on the line, to risk who you think you are in service to the unfolding expression of who you could be, or who you truly are when all self-protective mechanisms and self-concealing personality structures are stripped away. To play is to endure a plight and to pledge to remain true to yourself along the way, no matter what conditions you encounter. To play is to take an oath, swearing to enter the totality of experience offered by this life—from mourning to magic, labor to love—holding back nothing. For example, in Nazi-controlled concentration camps after 1939, "instead of playing tag, children played 'Gestapo, policemen, and Jews,' mimicking their current situation. There was a whole community effort to create parks and recreational activities to improve the morale of the camp's inhabitants, even when the situation was terrible. Play became a way to 'cope' with the terrible situation they were in."[13]

This emphasis on experience is key, because whatever play is, it is not theoretical. The cowherd maidens did not theoretically risk the disapproval and scorn of the families and friends they left behind when they ran feverishly through the dark to meet Krishna in that moonlit field. Musicians do not theoretically risk something when they pick up their flute and perform, emptying themselves enough to feel the wind of their inward divinity. Stepping into the groundlessness of music-making, venturing into that moonlit field, they allow the archetypal Krishna to move through and overcome them, overturning everything. And he makes a *plegan* to stay right there, in the agony of exposure, in the discomfort of that "pure, hollow note"[14] as it "spreads like lightning in all directions."[15]

To experience play, then, is to risk dissolving into union with a force so otherworldly, so beyond the knowable and mundane, that it seems to unite "mourning" and "love" as if by "sorcery." As Rumi writes in *The Reed Flute's Song:*

The reed flute
is fire, not wind. Be that empty.

Hear the love fire tangled
in the reed notes, as bewilderment

melts into wine. The reed is a friend
to all who want the fabric torn

and drawn away. The reed is hurt
and salve combining. Intimacy

and longing for intimacy, one
song. A disastrous surrender
and a fine love, together.[16]

INTO THE WINE-DARK SEA

This is the heart of the play experience: We stand before the threshold of the unknown, and say, along with Odysseus, "and what if one of the gods does wreck me out on the wine-dark sea? . . . let this new disaster come."[17] In fact, this connection between the experience of play and a perilous sea voyage is not just poetic, but also etymological: The word "experience" traces back to the Indo-European *per-*, "to attempt, venture, risk,"[18] the same root from which comes the Old English *faer*, meaning "danger, sudden calamity," giving rise to our modern word fear.[19] And *per-* appears again in the Greek word *peirates*, meaning "attacker," the source of our English word "pirate."[20] In its oldest associations, it means to go "forward, through," as in the Greek verb *perao*, meaning "I pass through."[21]

The experience of true play, then, is a perpetual risking, a movement through fear, a "pledge" to "pass through" a "perilous" journey, into the unknown, "binding" yourself to the center of your being and surrendering to those winds that "move lightly" and "quickly" as they dance across the waves. This latter meaning is contained, as well, in one of the

Sanskrit words for play, *krīdati*, which refers to the play of animals, children, and adults, as well as "the movement of wind or waves."[22]

In recent years, scientists have discovered a neurochemical basis for this connection between risk, fear, and the flow states characteristic of deep play. "Whenever we take a risk or identify a pattern," writes flow researcher Steven Kotler in *The Rise of Superman*, the brain releases dopamine, which we experience as an inrush of "excitement, engagement, and curiosity . . . it also tightens focus, drives us into the now, and, thus, speeds entrance into flow. What all of this means is that the creative act (one that requires risk-taking and pattern recognition) is itself an exceptionally potent flow trigger."[23] And this risk-taking necessarily requires us to move through fear, to treat fear even as "a compass," in Kotler's words, directing us toward the richest and most transformative arenas of play.[24]

Harvard psychiatrist Ned Hallowell corroborates this connection when he says that "to reach flow . . . one must be willing to take risks. The lover must lay bare his soul and risk rejection and humiliation to enter this state. The athlete must be willing to risk physical harm, even loss of life, to enter this state. The artist must be willing to be scorned and despised by the critics and still push on. And the average person— you and me—must be willing to fail, look foolish, and fall flat on our faces."[25]

Like Rumi's "disastrous surrender," this play is at its core a "longing for intimacy," for the fabric of separation to be "torn and drawn away" in the rapturous union of self and other, player and played. *Krīdati* therefore reappears as Krīdaratnam, the "jewel of games," referring to the erotic play of lovemaking.[26] This association between play and a certain flavor of eroticism is universal: The Blackfoot stem *koani* refers to both children's games and illicit relationships;[27] the German word *"spielkind"* means "a child born out of wedlock" and is connected to the Dutch word *"aanspelen,"* "the mating of dogs"[28]; and both are connected to the Swedish word *"leka"* "the coupling of birds," as is the English word "lechery,"[29] which the Oxford English Dictionary defines as "excessive or offensive sexual desire."

THE EROTIC NATURE OF PLAY

To play Erotically is to move beyond the bounds, outside of or between the conventional distinctions of right and wrong. In a tension of opposites, it is to suffer a paradox, to endure an ambiguity, and to allow a force that is at once elemental and spiritual to course through and animate that in-between space.

Consider the exquisite torture of an only-somewhat-requited love: How her every subtle glance can seem to rearrange the cosmos; how the thought of him washes your skin in hot, electric streams of sweat; and the softness of a smile that fills a lifetime of emptiness. Would this torture be as sweet without that spark that burns where maybe-one-day meets but-maybe-never? With every flicker of an opening, this tension pulls apart our pride and carries us along its path one "maybe" at a time.

This brings us to the true meaning of that wrongfully trivialized word for play, "entertainment," which derives from the Old French *entretenir,* meaning "held in-between," or "to create . . . a liminal space."[30] In its original usage, the word means to consider a third possibility, between right and wrong, good and bad, self and other—to entertain the mystery of a union of opposites, that state of grace the alchemists called the *mysterium coniunctionis* and outstretched themselves toward eternally as if it were a distant lighthouse on a perilous sea.

And in the moment of contact, when the distinctions between self and other fall away, we spontaneously encounter another play-word:

recreation. "Play is called recreation," writes Dr. Stuart Brown, "because it makes us new again, it recreates us and our world."[31] Play melts down the habitual and the known, allowing us to see the world and our place in it with sudden clarity, unfettered by cultural baggage and childhood conditioning.

New neural pathways form as we immerse ourselves into life with the recognition that it wants only to play with us. And as we venture beyond the prison of our identity—whose iron bars were forged from the shaming voices of our upbringing—we discover, to our astonishment, that there was nothing to fear all along. Like the Bengali poet Rabindranath Tagore, we encounter "the waves of creation" and realize that "these risings and fallings are not the erratic contortions of disparate bodies, they are a rhythmic dance." And we throw ourselves joyously into this dance—into that mystery through which mourning and music, magic and love are bound in the ecstasy of their play. This is what we mean when we say that play is a pathway to the sacred. Play is a deep and primal biological drive, with its roots in our evolutionary history. And it is a mindset, an orientation to life, through which we transcend that history while firmly connected to the animal in us.

THE ELEMENTS OF PLAY

Having established play as a state of mind, an orientation to reality, a biological drive, and a creative mystery, let's now explore its essential elements. What does it feel like, subjectively, when we are in touch with this mystery, when this drive is activated, when we encounter our world with a playful orientation?

In his book *Play: How It Shapes the Brain, Opens the Imagination, and Invigorates the Soul,* Dr. Stuart Brown outlines seven properties he sees as fundamental to the play experience, namely, that it is apparently purposeless, voluntary, inherently attractive, provides freedom from time, diminished consciousness of self, improvisational potential, and continuation desire.[32] Revising and expanding his list, we have arrived at the following eight elements of our own: for us, play is autotelic, voluntary, fun, and characterized by the desire to continue, diminished self-consciousness, time dilation, optionality, and possession.

PLAY IS AUTOTELIC

This first element of play—that it is autotelic or done for its own sake—speaks to the main distinction between play and what so many consider to be its opposite: work. The defining characteristic of work is that it is done for an end other than itself. We work to survive, to support a family, to get rich, to demonstrate our competence. Much like when God tells Adam and Eve in that Biblical punishment in Genesis 3:17, "You will get your food . . . only by labor all the days of your life . . . and only by the sweat of your brow will you win your bread," we are accustomed to treating work as a burdensome, even punitive, activity. And when we work for the joy and pleasure of the work itself, when we offer ourselves entirely to a labor of love, we enter another domain in which the term "work" falls short.

We have all met people so fueled and energized by their work that they would rather be doing it than anything else in the world. These people find themselves continually challenged to expand—to become more complex, adaptive, creative, resourceful, and engaged—throughout their work lives. Like the mechanic who spends hours joyously tinkering under the hood, or the physician who treats each patient as a creative challenge, an opportunity to deepen their capacity for compassion and reciprocal healing, there are people who derive a sense of deep enjoyment from their work, incompatible with the intentions of that biblical punishment. Their vocation becomes a channel through which they can most fully express themselves and play with life. These people experience a sense of *funkionslust,* a German word that refers to the joy of performing an activity for its own sake, the joy of having your inner brilliance and natural gifts drawn out and utilized during the course of your activity. This quality of *funkionslust* is enough to transform even the most mundane or tedious labor into a delightful act of play.

Certain communities, such as those found in traditional, remote villages in the European alps, have even gone so far as to structure their lifestyles entirely around this *funkionslust* experience. In the late 1980s, a team of Italian psychologists led by Professor Fausto Massimini and Dr. Antonella Delle Fave traveled throughout the alps to interview elderly people who still lived in some of these communities. Summarizing their findings, the University of Chicago psychologist and flow research pioneer Mihaly Csikszentmihalyi writes in *Flow: The Psychology of Optimal Experience*:

> The most striking feature of such places is that those who live there can seldom distinguish work from free time. It could be said that they work sixteen hours each day, but then it could also be argued that they never work. One of the inhabitants, Serafina Vinon, a seventy-six-year-old woman from the tiny hamlet of Pont Trentaz, in the Valle d'Aosta region of the Italian Alps, still gets up at five in the morning to milk her cows. Afterward she cooks a huge breakfast, cleans the house, and, depending on the weather and time of year, either takes the herd to the meadows just below the glaciers, tends the orchard, or cards some wool. In summer she spends weeks on the high pastures cutting hay, and then carries huge bales of it on her head the several miles down to the barn. She could reach the barn in half the time if she took a

direct route; but she prefers following invisible winding trails to save the slopes from erosion. . . .

When Serafina was asked what she enjoys doing most in life, she had no trouble answering: milking the cows, taking them to the pasture, pruning the orchard, carding wool . . . in effect, what she enjoys most is what she has been doing for a living all along. In her own words: "It gives me a great satisfaction. To be outdoors, to talk with people, to be with my animals . . . too bad that you get tired and have to go home . . . even when you have to work a lot it is very beautiful."[33]

Serafina's story shows how manual labor, when approached with an autotelic orientation, can evoke a sense of *funkionslust*—of total engagement, absorption, and delight. Here again, we find that play is a matter of context rather than content, of the spirit with which an activity is performed rather than the concrete facts of the experience itself.

PLAY IS VOLUNTARY, OR FREELY CHOSEN

The next element of play is that it is voluntary, or freely chosen. In the words of philosopher James Carse, "It is an invariable principle of all play . . . that whoever plays, plays freely. Whoever must play, cannot play."[34] Put another way, we could say that play can never occur within a context of compulsion. The moment we try to compel behavior, we disturb the intrinsic motivational structure that is the lifeblood of the play experience. We move from a state of *funkionslust* to one of *endlust*—from a state of rapt absorption and penetrating involvement to a state of anxiously monitoring and evaluating whether our behavior will earn us the approval, or at least shield us from the disapproval, of those whom we have made into authority figures.

It makes no difference whether these authority figures are externalized as teachers, employers, or peers, or internalized as the critical voices in our head. In either case, we are cleaved from the object of our play, from the immediacy of our felt experience. And as we lust for the end, for the termination of the game—which we imagine also to be the termination of our evaluation period—our attention strays from the scene of our play to the person we believe is evaluating our performance within that scene. We become increasingly displaced and dissociated from our activity, as parts of ourselves remain outside of the play itself, judging our increasingly affected and unspontaneous behavior.

As a result, we engage in our activity with a fractured self, a fragmented representation of who we truly are. This may present as a total creative paralysis, in which our capacity to play is imprisoned by our fear of playing "wrongly," or it may present as excessively flashy, pumped-up behavior. Either way, we are estranged from ourselves. Our essential nature, and how it most yearns to express itself, becomes distorted, obscured, and made clumsy by the density of filters it must contort itself to pass through. Under the anticipated threat of judgment, we lose the capacity to freely relate and engage as whole persons. Our actions cease to be overflowing expressions of love and instead become emaciated petitions for love.

Those who can recall their middle school dance know the difference between dancing to look good and dancing for the fun of it. When the stakes are this high, we can feel terribly vulnerable when we express ourselves honestly; for what if we expose who we truly are and are then rejected for it?

But if we follow Miles Davis's instruction to "not fear mistakes, [as] there are none,"[35] we may find that our true expression draws others toward us, especially when that expression reveals something awkward, uncalculated, embarrassing. For there is something attractive about unabashedly approving of our own flaws and imperfections.

Seeking only the pleasure of this revelation—of discovering our true nature, and the true nature of those around us, through the course of our play—we begin to relish the unveiling of even that which we had judged and felt ashamed of, of the parts of ourselves we had not given the space to breathe and stretch their limbs. In doing so, we naturally invite others to reveal themselves as well.

As we play to come into relationship with ourselves—to experience intimacy with who we are and share that intimacy with those around us—we find that the conditions under which we are willing to risk playing naturally expand. In every moment of "even here," we recollect a part of ourselves we had left behind during our years of approval-seeking. We reclaim a patch of terrain, a landscape of experience that, out of fear, we had barred ourselves from. We begin to relate to others as whole people, rather than as screens for our projected self-doubt and insecurity. Instead of compelling them to play along in our drama, we can inspire others to risk revealing who they truly are, as we risk revealing who we truly are.

PLAY IS FUN

We again encounter one of those "I know it when I see it" situations.

Whatever fun is, we recognize it intuitively as the heart of the play experience. If what we're doing isn't fun, it likely isn't play. Stuart Brown tells the story of traveling to Alaska's Admiralty Island with Dr. Bob Fagen, the world's foremost expert on animal play. As they watched a couple bears play-wrestling and splashing through nearby pools, he asked:

"Bob, why do these animals play?"

After some hesitation, Dr. Fagen replied: "Because it's fun."[36]

This answer, brief as it is, somehow feels more complete than the longer explanation he later gave after more prying ("in a world continually presenting unique challenges and ambiguity, play prepares these bears for an evolving planet"[37]). Evolutionary benefits notwithstanding, play is play because it's fun, and that's why we love to do it. And as long as our play continues to be fun, we won't ever want to stop.

THE DESIRE TO CONTINUE

This brings us to our next element of play: the desire to continue. Simply put, those who play desire to keep playing. This, again, is intuitive. If an activity is intrinsically rewarding, freely chosen, and fun, then why would anyone want to stop? As players, we may even go so far as to renegotiate our boundaries, taking them into the arena of our play, if those boundaries threaten the continuation of the game. Although this removal of barriers may constitute a risk, it is a risk we are willing to take.

We find, in fact, that every genuine moment of play is interwoven with this risk. With each moment of contact with our instrument—embracing the smooth wood of the guitar's neck as it slides across our palm—we encounter a new aspect of ourselves, or encounter an aspect of ourselves anew, drawing us deeper into intimacy with ourselves and with life. The ending of our play, then, is a return to the concerns of survival and commerce. The French say that "the aim of desire is not its satisfaction, but its prolongation,"[38] and, as players, we want nothing more than to prolong our love-making with this life: to melt down the identity, with all its fears and withholds, and reforge ourselves in the heat of recreation, recasting ourselves in the image of our original nature, which is love. The discovery of what we are capable of is the motivation for prolonging and continuing to play.

DIMINISHED SELF-CONSCIOUSNESS

In the words of T. S. Eliot, every creative move is "a step to the block, to the fire, down the sea's throat."[39] When in deep states of play, we are electrified by an elemental power, at once both spiritual and physical. Our whole being turns white hot, too hot for our little ego to hang on to, and as it slips away, we experience a temporary relief from the burden of having to continually fortify our self-image, of having to defend ourselves mentally from the perceived threats in our social environment. In play, we continually and deliberately undermine our dependency on these protections as we surrender to the deeper expression that wants to come through. This results in a paradox: The less we cling to ourselves, the more we encounter ourselves. As our self-consciousness slips away from our awareness, our true self expands to take its place, delighted by its sudden liberation from the limiting confines of our identity. We make fresh contact with our environment, feeling the subtle textures of the gravel beneath our shoes, and allowing the wind's touch to send shivers down our spine. Every moment of unfettered intimacy between self and other plunges us deeper into this state: the fragrance of our lover and the gentle rumblings of an earthquake pull us toward that vanishing point in which self and environment converge. As one long-distance sailor put it, here, "one forgets oneself, one forgets everything, seeing only the play of the boat with the sea, the play of the sea around the boat, leaving aside everything not essential to that game."[40]

This experience of diminished self-consciousness is characterized by a temporary deactivation of parts of the prefrontal cortex (PFC), what neuroscientists call *transient hypofrontality*. The American University of Beirut professor Arne Dietrich describes this as "an efficiency exchange. We're trading energy usually used for higher cognitive functions for heightened attention and awareness."[41]

And the nature of our experience is determined by which regions of the PFC are deactivated. "The greater the deactivation of neuronal structures," writes Kotler, "the more profound . . . the experience."[42]

One study performed by a team of Israeli scientists in 2006, for example, found that "When people lose themselves in a task . . . a part of the superior frontal gyrus starts to deactivate."[43] This structure is involved in the generation of self-consciousness—the maintenance of that defended identity, which is the primary impediment to immersion into an experience. When this part of the brain goes offline, we can engage in activity without reflecting on or evaluating it. The researchers concluded their paper by stating that "during intense perceptual engagement . . . the distracting self-related cortex is inactive. Thus, the term 'losing yourself' receives here a clear neuronal correlate. This theme has a tantalizing echoing in Eastern philosophies such as Zen teachings, which emphasize the need to enter into a . . . selfless mental state to achieve a true sense of reality."[44]

Another study at Johns Hopkins University used fMRI (functional magnetic resonance imaging) scans to look at what happens in the brains of jazz musicians and freestyle rappers when they improvise. Charles Limb, the head of the study, discovered that the dorsolateral prefrontal cortex, which is responsible for "self-monitoring and impulse control," deactivates during these experiences of improvisational flow.[45] It is this dissolution of self-consciousness, combined with the inhibition of impulse control, that liberates the deeper self, allowing our true nature to come through and express itself.

TIME DILATION

When we are swept up in this kind of play, hours can pass in what feels like minutes, and minutes can seem to go on for days. In the psychological literature, this phenomenon is referred to as *time dilation*—the transformation of our subjective experience of time. As it turns out, the neurological mechanism underlying this experience also happens to involve hypofrontality (decreased blood flow in the prefrontal cortex). After performing a series of fMRI experiments, the Baylor University neuroscientist David Eagleman (now at Stanford University) discovered that our awareness of time is calculated by multiple parts of the prefrontal cortex working together simultaneously. And, because large parts of the PFC go offline during deep play, our ability to perform this calculation becomes inhibited. "Energy normally used for temporal processing is reallocated for attention and awareness," writes Kotler. "Instead of keeping time, we are taking in more data per second . . . it is all this data that actually elongates the current moment. Our sense of how long 'the now' lasts is related to information processing."[46]

When in these deep states of play, we connect with a rhythm, a pulse that occurs as deeper and truer than the contrivances of clock time. The Greeks referred to this deeper time as *kairos,* and distinguished it from the chronological time of *chronos.* The latter consists of objectively measured, linear intervals, while the former consists of subjectively experienced feeling tones, more akin to the time at which a season changes, or the time to lean in and kiss a lover.

The ancient Taoists called the innermost self an "unsculpted block of time,"[47] as the deeper we are drawn into the essence of our being, the more we are liberated from the conditioned time of *chronos* and thrown into the immediacy of *kairos.* Time begins to melt, warp, and bend when refracted through the prism of our being, that unsculpted block of time that is anterior to all calendrics. In the timeless time of *kairos,* the only time is now, and the only thing that matters is how we meet this cosmic rhythm, how willing we are to say, like Ella Fitzgerald, that

"It don't mean a thing if it ain't got that swing" and throw ourselves into the dance.

OPTIONALITY

To understand this next element of play, we will turn (of all places!) to the world of finance, specifically the domain of options trading. A financial option confers the right, but not the obligation, to buy or sell some underlying asset at a predetermined price over a specified period. To illustrate how this works, let's examine the story of Thales's olive presses, which, according to options-trader-turned-philosopher Nassim Taleb, recounts the first options trade in history.

Thales was a Greek-speaking, pre-Socratic philosopher and mathe-matician from the coastal town of Miletus, a trading post in Asia Minor. Having grown tired of his more commercially minded friends' teasing, he "put a down payment on the seasonal use of every olive press in the vicinity of Miletus and Chios, which he got at low rent. The harvest turned out to be extremely bountiful and there was demand for olive presses, so he released the owners of olive presses on his own terms, building a substantial fortune in the process. Then he went back to philosophizing."[48]

For Taleb, and Montaigne before him, this story holds the antidote to Aesop's "The Fox and the Grapes" fable. The latter tells of a fox who tries repeatedly to reach a bunch of grapes and, after failing to do so, announces that they were not worth having in the first place. Thales, on the contrary, proves to his friends and to himself that he *could* be a wealthy merchant if he wanted to, but *preferred* to spend his time philosophizing. He had the option—the right, but not the obligation—to enter and thrive in the mercantile world.

Working along these lines, we can define optionality as the capacity to spot hidden options or otherwise untapped resources in our environment; to discern opportunities for creative action, available but not obligatory; and the freedom to choose how to engage those opportunities. According to Taleb, "financial options may be expensive because people know they are options and someone is selling them and charging a price—but most interesting options are free, or at the worst, cheap."[49]

By simply shifting our perspective and keeping our attention open and unburdened by preconceptions, we can discover creative possibilities, alternative outcomes, and novel solutions to old problems. But this requires the presence of mind to notice the habitual grooves of our patterned responses, as well as the power to shake ourselves free from them and choose a new direction.

Consider the discovery of penicillin. Alexander Fleming, a Scottish microbiologist and physician who had been somewhat disorderly in his laboratory protocols, returned from a holiday in 1928 to discover that a fungus, *Penicillium notatum,* had contaminated a culture plate of *Staphylococcus* bacteria he had accidentally left uncovered. Rather than chastising himself for his negligence, he increased his attention and noticed that the bacteria had disappeared in precisely those areas where the fungus had grown. Upon further experimentation with this fungus, Fleming discovered that it was effective even at extremely diluted concentrations. He then partnered with British pharmaceutical companies to produce the first widely available antibiotic, saving countless lives.[50]

Fleming's case is instructive. Our willingness to set down our plans and change with life's surprises often allow for more creativity, beauty, and healing than those original plans would have ever allowed for. Intuitively, we know this: When we lose a job, or otherwise experience a sudden change in circumstance, we're often told by those closest to us that, in time, we'll end up finding something even better—a more exciting job, a more fulfilling relationship. And, more often than not, this turns out to be the case: When life takes what we had singularly clung to, we can recognize the richness of opportunity that surrounds us.

As these stories illustrate, optionality is essential to a playful approach to life. We don't need to know what's going to happen next. We just need the presence of mind to notice, and then exercise, the option when it presents itself—to walk through an unexpected door when it appears. We can rest assured that no matter how far we stray from our initial goals, and no matter what mistakes we make along the way, we could never get lost on our journey, because these deviations and unexpected turns are themselves taken into the play and experienced as sources of inspiration. Our accidents become invitations to play in otherwise unrecognized or unexpected directions. The more we free our attention, decoupling it from anticipated outcomes, the more we can discover these creative opportunities in our environment.

The French biologist Francois Jacob has even suggested that this kind of optionality is the primary mechanism by which evolution unfolds. In an essay titled "Evolution and Tinkering," Jacob writes: "The action of natural selection has often been compared to that of an engineer. This, however, does not seem to be a suitable comparison. First, because in contrast to what occurs in evolution, the engineer works according to a preconceived plan in that he foresees the product of his efforts. Second, because of the way the engineer works: to make a new product, he has at his disposal both material specially prepared to that end and machines designed solely for that task."[51]

In contrast to this engineering metaphor, Jacob suggests that it is more appropriate to compare the process of evolution to the workings of a tinkerer. "Often, without any well-defined long-term project," he writes, "the tinkerer gives his material unexpected functions to produce a new object. From an old bicycle wheel, he makes roulette; from a broken chair the cabinet of a radio. Similarly, evolution makes a wing from a leg or a part of an ear from a piece of jaw . . . evolution does not produce novelties from scratch. It works on what already exists, either transforming a system to give it new functions or combining several systems to produce a more elaborate one."[52]

Jacob uses the French word *bricolage* to describe this optionality-like tinkering process. Bricolage is the process of taking whatever is available and playing with it, messing around through trial and error to generate creative novelty. Like a golden retriever, who can play fetch with any old shoe; or a grandma, who can make mouthwatering meals out of a few leftover scrap ingredients; or a five-year-old girl who can see, in an old willow branch, a witch's wand; bricolage is the repurposing of unwanted, unintentional, or discarded material, taking whatever is at hand and turning it into magic.

One of the most potent mythological portrayals of bricolage can be found in the opening of *The Homeric Hymn to Hermes,* which tells the story of how the young trickster god created the first musical instrument. Rolling out of his cradle, the unruly infant Hermes stumbled across a turtle and talked it into returning with him to his cave. He then "turned her over and with a scoop of gray iron scraped the marrow from her mountain shell. And, just as a swift thought can fly through the heart of a person haunted with care, just as bright glances spin from the eyes, so, in one instant, Hermes knew what to do and did it. He cut stalks of reed to measure, fitted them through the shell, and fastened their ends across the back. Skillfully, he tightened a piece of cowhide, set the arms in place, fixed a yoke across them, and stretched seven sheep-gut strings to sound in harmony." And so the lyre, which "rang out beautifully at the touch of his hand," came to be.[53]

PLAYING WITH WORLDS

As we continue to widen our horizons of possibility, we discover that, with sufficient creativity, any number of realities can be composed from the same set of facts. By recombining facts and worldviews the way sexual selection reshuffles genetic material, we can participate creatively in the birth of new worlds, adding the imaginative power of our consciousness to the play of universes arising and dissolving. This mythopoesis, this cosmological bricolage, is in fact the traditional role of the Lila poet. "In the boundless universe of poetry, the poet is creator,"[54] writes the ninth-century mystic Anandavardhana, "and as it pleases him, so does this world come forth." And "triumphant is the word of the poet," writes the eleventh-century Sanskrit philosopher Mammata, "which creates a world."[55]

John Reed, the former CEO of Citicorp, one of the largest banks in the world, speaks to this kind of optionality when he says: "I don't think there is such a thing as reality. There are widely varying descriptions of reality, and you've got to be alert to when they change and what's going on. No one is going to truly grasp it, but you have to stay truly active on that end. That implies you have to have a multifaceted perspective . . . there is a set of realities that exist at any moment in time. I always have some kind of model in my mind as to what I think is going on in the world. I'm always tuning that [model] and trying to get different insights."[56]

But, when taken too far, this plurality of worlds, of noncommittal options, can weaken our focus. We can get caught in the in-between, the *entretenir* of entertainment in its negative form. Eventually, we must choose a reality, as well as a course of action within that reality, while always remembering that we have consciously and decisively chosen it. By electing to restrict our options, we can penetrate deeper into our environment, discerning subtler, more nuanced opportunities for action.

Paradoxically, by freely throwing up blinders, by narrowing our aperture, we can accentuate our vision. Previously invisible options become visible as we squeeze ourselves into this voluntary confinement. By stretching our body and our mind to its limits, we activate a deeper resourcefulness and inner knowing than would otherwise have been accessible. Optionality is the opposite of victim consciousness: The latter assumes we are helplessly at the mercy of a life that imposes its will upon us involuntarily; the former remembers that, at any moment, no matter the circumstances, inner freedom is a choice. And should we choose to play the victim to life, we will remember that that, too, is a choice.

Through optionality we arrive at a paradoxical union of total freedom and total constraint. We become utterly involved in our play, committing entirely to its limits and its rules, while retaining the option to modify our outlook when those limits threaten to terminate the continuation of the game. Should we approach a dead end, we know we can choose to play with those limits just as freely as we had previously played within them.

THE WAY TO OPTIONALITY

When it comes to deepening our access to optionality, we have four tools at our disposal: attention, approval, intimacy, and intuition. By widening and deepening our attention, we can spot hidden options, latent opportunities for creative action, and un-potentiated resources in our environment. By meeting our circumstances with approval, irrespective of how pleasurable or unpleasurable they may be, we recover a sense of agency over our experience: We may not like what is happening, but we can at least choose whether to opt in, knowing that doing so will free up energy for our play.

From here, we can make intimate contact with our environment, sensing its contours, feeling its textures on our skin, attuning ourselves to its rhythms and yearnings, including the way it outstretches itself, inviting us in to play. And we can outstretch ourselves in return, exposing our vulnerabilities such that we are touched at the level of the soul in every moment of our engagement. This intimacy is our only goal, this meeting of souls, this union with our environment.

This is how we open up our intuition: We become intimate with unspoken desires in the moment as they arise between us and the environment, between self and other. From this state of surrendered receptivity, we allow ourselves to be guided deeper into the mystery of the moment, beneath the constructs of socially conditioned responses, into the pulsing veins of unconditioned reality. To hear and respond to this inner guidance, we cast aside prejudices, biases, or assumptions. Intuition gives us sight into the mystery of creation, as well as the moment-by-moment directions we need to participate in that mystery. It allows us to see through the artifice of performed roles into the art of creative living. Casting aside scripts and preconceptions, all habituated and formulaic ways of relating to a scene, we listen inwardly for the next right play and allow ourselves to be surprised by what we hear. "You've got to be kidding me," we think, "I can't say *that.*" In time, as our relationship with this inner guidance deepens, we allow ourselves to be not only directed but taken, not only guided but possessed. We move from simply taking dictation to being overcome by the source of that dictation, by some deeper wisdom. Taking this wisdom as our *magister ludi* (a reference to Hermann Hesse's *The Glass Bead Game*), our inward game master, we allow ourselves to be directed toward and initiated deeper into divine play.

The horizons of unscripted potentiality in our lives widen as we discover that there is no circumstance this wisdom could not provide the answer to—even if its answer is to drop the answer-seeking mind and instead commit ourselves deeper to the back-and-forth questioning, to the probing of the inexhaustible mystery that is this unfolding life. "Be patient toward all that is unsolved in your heart," writes Rainer Maria Rilke, "and try to love the questions themselves like locked rooms and like books that are written in a very foreign tongue . . . live the questions now. Perhaps you will then gradually, without noticing it, live along some distant day into the answer."[57]

POSSESSION

Who, then, is this inward guide? Who whispers to us as our intuition? Who moves through us and throws us limb by limb into the dance of God? Who are these elemental powers, electric and alive, that charge us with the demiurgic necessity to create?

In pre-Islamic Arabia, they were called *al-Jinn,* and were known to inhabit certain places and attach themselves to oracles, philosophers, and poets, directing every syllable as their words spilled forth involuntarily in ecstatic outbursts of surrender.[58] The ancient Romans rendered this term in Latin as the *genii*—or *genius* in the singular—and believed that "even places in a landscape or fields or groves could possess their *genius,* the *genius loci* . . . used in this way, the word *genius* referred more to the psychic atmosphere or to the mood that such a place can evoke."[59]

Consider the moonlit field to which the flute-playing Krishna drew those maidens, how in some sense their rapturous dance could only have occurred right there in that place, concomitant with the spirit that presided over it. And then consider that the unity of your body, mind, and soul itself constitutes a kind of place, an ambiance, a field, with its own presiding spirit, its own genius, summoning you to a creative life. The eighth-century Buddhist sage Saraha said that "here in this body are the sacred rivers: here are the sun and moon as well as the pilgrimage places."[60] And the genius is the spirit that calls this body its home. It is the one that draws the sacred rivers of the soul into a unity, channeling the body and the psyche into a singular force of creative nature.

The American dancer Martha Graham spoke to this force when she said: "There is a vitality, a life force, an energy, a quickening, that is translated through you into action, and because there is only one of you in all time, this expression is unique. And if you block it, it will never exist through any medium and will be lost."[61] Genius is the generative force, the power that moves through us in moments of creative possession, electrifying us with the urge to physicalize the spiritual, to articulate the ineffable, to ensnare in chiseled stone a form that chose us as its midwife. When we are possessed by this spirit, we can say, along with Michelangelo, that "I saw the angel in the marble and carved until I set him free."[62] In the reeling intoxication of this possession, we are at once the carved and the carver, the liberator and the liberated. In this play of creation, our genius re-creates us in its own image, cleaving us from the suffocating weight of conventions, expectations, preconceptions, and rationalizations.

Play evokes a deeper, more authentic *us*, as a force more powerful than convention that would mute us.

IN MODERN USAGE, the term "genius" has come to refer to an innately talented individual. But in premodern times, people unanimously drew a distinction between the spirit of genius and the individual that spirit had chosen to inhabit and play through. The memoirist Elizabeth Gilbert speaks to this distinction in her TED Talk when she tells of the traditional moonlit dances that took place in North Africa centuries ago. Every once in a while, one of these dancers would step through an invisible door into another world. And "all of a sudden, he would no longer appear to be merely human. He would be lit from within, and lit from below, and all lit up on fire with divinity. . . . Back then, people knew it for what it was, they called it by its name. They would put their hands together, and they would start to chant, 'Allah, Allah, Allah, God, God, God'. . . . When the Moors invaded southern Spain, they took this custom with them, and the pronunciation changed over time from 'Allah, Allah, Allah,' to 'Olé, Olé, Olé,' which you still hear in bullfights and in flamenco dances."[63]

This rapturous state of divine possession is the hallmark of deep play. Whatever we choose to name this force—whether *jinn* or *genius,* Allah or the Muse—its presence is unmistakable. And when we surrender ourselves entirely to the play of its creative force, we remember our divinity, not as a thought, but as an embodied experience. We dissolve into the tumultuous dance of creation and intuitively hear each note as it swings itself out of the sacred. This is why the word "music" derives etymologically from the Muse: Every moment of creation is underwritten with rhythm, and the Muse is the one who beckons us to pick up our instruments and accompany this celestial harmony with our own unique melody.[64] And each time we do so, each time we enter into total participation with this unfolding Lila, we are renewed, revitalized, restored to ourselves, and so redeemed. The veil is pulled from our eyes, the rug is yanked from under our feet, and we can howl in laughter at the remembrance of our divinity. For a flash in time, we are in on the joke and can enjoy the game of hide-and-seek.

3

The Hunt for Consciousness

"Play is the hobgoblin of animal behavior, mischievously tempting us to succeed in what, judging from the number of failed attempts, seems a futile task: defining play."[1]

—ROBERT MITCHELL

"Nonhuman nature is the outward and visible expression of the mystery which confronts us when we look into the depths of our own being."[2]

—ALDOUS HUXLEY

PLAYING WITH BIOLOGY

Not content to limit himself to the narrow range of human experience, the god of Lila takes the form of every species in the universe. One text tells us that "the Lord manifested Himself as a boar, that He might enjoy playing in waters." Another says that "like an actor acting on a stage, He assumed and renounced His different forms, such as . . . fish and other [species]."[3]

When we look around the natural world, we can see that this play is everywhere—from the highest primates to the lowest insects. Ravens slip and slide through the snow on their backs and hippos do backflips. Grizzly bears play-fight for fun and bison slide around on frozen lakes.[4] Halfbeak fish do somersaults and turtles swim through hoops. "Even insects play together," writes Darwin, observing that "on fine, calm days, when they are feeling no hunger or . . . cause for anxiety, certain ants entertain themselves with sham fights, without doing each other any harm."[5]

The science research into this animal play behavior provides us with an immense treasure trove of information, allowing us to move from the ineffable worlds of metaphysics and mythology into the concrete domains of evolutionary biology and neuroscience, with all their precision and rigor. By exploring this information, we can evaluate claims of the Lila myth that the natural world is inherently playful. And we can use the evidence science provides to deepen our understanding of who we are and where we come from as playing animals, exploring how play has shaped our physiological, neurological, and psychological development across the broad sweep of evolutionary time.

But, we must admit, there is something a bit dry and unsatisfying about taking scientific literature at face value. Because science itself is conducted within the context of the myth of seriousness, biasing both its observations and its conclusions. To free ourselves from this seriousness, then, it will not be enough to merely discuss the science of play. Our game will be to play *with* the boundaries of science and not just *within* the boundaries of science. Equally fair game are the observations of Darwin and the indigenous folklore that predates his realizations by a millennia. There is innovative neuroscience and fringe theology, all offering their respective viewpoints for us to engage in and navigate our own investigation.

Because, as we will come to see, science is not an eternal and immutable monolith, standing outside of nature and observing it from above like the Biblical God after which it is unconsciously patterned. It is a deeply human pursuit, an outgrowth of the same playful forces through which nature organizes and becomes aware of herself.

THE BAIT THIEF AND THE EATING GAME

Let's start by diving back into the trickster archetype—that preeminent disruptor of boundaries. In the Lila myth, Krishna creates the world as an expression of his divine play, and he continually undermines its boundaries, categories, and constraints, removing impediments to the free flow of this play.

In the Native American context, the trickster also creates the world. But here, the archetype appears not as a divine child, but as an animal—typically a raven, rabbit, or coyote. The trickster's actions are motivated by his ambivalent relationship to his appetite, and the categories he most disrupts are those of "predator" and "prey" or "hunter" and "hunted."

The following fragment of a native Alaskan Tlingit story is typical in this regard:

> [Raven] came to a place where many people were encamped fishing. . . . He entered a house and asked what they used for bait. They said, "fat." Then he said, "Let me see you put enough on your hooks for bait." And he noticed carefully how they baited and handled their hooks. The next time they went out, he walked off behind a point and went underwater to get this bait. Now they got bites and pulled up quickly, but there was nothing on their hooks.[6]

Here, the raven is neither the hunter nor the hunted, but a third position that emerges between and because of the dynamic tension of the two. "He feeds his belly while standing just outside of the conflict," writes mythologist Lewis Hyde. "From that position the bait thief becomes a kind of critic of the usual rules of the eating game and as such subverts them."[7] His way, the third way, is related to the instinctual drives of appetite and procreation that run throughout the natural world—other trickster tales tell of his voracious sexuality—without being bound by or determined by those drives.

Sometimes, his play does in fact satisfy one of these biological imperatives. Other times, his antics backfire, leaving him hungry, embarrassed, or even dead. But taken together, the animal trickster's behavior illustrates the process by which creative intelligence refines itself, through the interplay of an alternatingly slightly smarter prey evading a slightly smarter predator.

The trickster's way inserts flexibility into the rigidity of fixed, instinctual reactions—of static predator-prey dynamics—and generates novelty, adaptability, ingenuity, and freedom. He tests the limits of his biology and finds where those limits break or bend, where hardwired behaviors begin to wobble. This playing with his biology, testing the limits and constraints on his behavior, is his highest aim: not just to eat, but to see how far he can exit the hunting game while keeping his belly full.

THE ANIMAL AS OTHER

The mythology of the animal trickster is instructive for our attempts to approach biology playfully. For the trickster begins in a world of survival needs, of hunter and hunted, life and death, and ends up inverting that world through play. He does not take his survival seriously and instead approaches it playfully, seeing what he can do with it, how much he can mess with its rules, and how much fun he can have along the way. In the mythology of the animal trickster, nature itself begins to realize that it is playing a game, and that it is free to choose how to relate to that game.

This story begins 85 million years ago in a world shrouded in darkness. It centers around an unlikely protagonist, from humble beginnings: a small, nocturnal tree shrew living on the forest floors of Africa. This hero—whose descendants would, over millions of years, evolve into our primate ancestors, and eventually into modern humans—lived in a world of pregnant darkness, of movement and sound, texture and smell. A world so dark that vision was largely useless. And so, he was nearly blind, having to orient himself by sniffing the ground for the fragrance of food or the pheromones of predators, while keeping his ears alert to the sound of danger amid the cacophony of jungle noises.[8]

Over time, he and his children and his children's children developed a complex catalog of remembered sounds and smells with which they could discern sensory patterns in their environment, establishing which sounds and smells were friendly, and which spelled danger. "It required a good brain to hold [those patterns] in mind," writes the ecologist Paul Shepard in *The Others*, "marking the creation of an auditory world in which rhythms and musical phrases such as the successive notes of birdsong are heard as a melody."[9]

Who knows what moved the descendants of this ancestor shrew to venture beyond the familiar world of darkness and ascend into the trees, climbing along branches outstretched toward the sun. But ascend they did, carrying with them the neural networks that had allowed them to structure a chaotic world of scent and noise into a harmonic symphony of music and perfume. The paleontologist Loren Eiseley called this *time-binding*: The ability to arrange sensory information into chronological patterns. As they habituated to their new arboreal environment, these early mammals reorganized their neurology, transferring the function of their sound and smell memory systems to their eyes, time-binding their sense impressions into a chronology of images.[10]

It is here, in the treetops, that the serpent wisdom first appears onto the scene. For as the evolutionary biologist Lynne Isbell has shown, the ancient primates that evolved from these shrews developed color vision largely as a result of their encounters with snakes. In her book *The Fruit, the Tree, and the Serpent: Why We See So Well*, she points out that "visual systems are more developed in those primates that have shared the longest evolutionary time with venomous snakes and least developed in those primates that have had no exposure at all to venomous snakes."[11]

This makes sense: Primates with vivid color vision could more easily detect camouflaged snakes in their environment, and so would have a survival advantage over those with poorer vision. Unlike other nearby mammals, our primate ancestors were most active in the daytime and had ample exposure to the light shining through their treetop environment. Venomous serpents, then, provided the precise adaptive pressures necessary for our evolutionary ancestors to restructure and expand their visual systems, initiating them into a world of vibrant color.[12]

Having detected a nearby snake in the environment, as social animals, our primate ancestors' next impulse would be to communicate that discovery. Here, too, they created novel ways to play the game of survival by discovering that they could point to the danger. It turns out that humans are unique in their ability to point declaratively—that is, to point out an object to get someone else interested in it. Other animals can point imperatively, to draw attention to something the pointer is interested in. But we are the only ones who can point in order to share interest in an object.[13]

This, too, likely developed as a result of our ancestors' cohabitation with snakes. "Because more eyes are more effective at spotting danger," writes Isbell, "the chance of seeing a snake before stepping too near to it would have increased with others around. Declarative pointing undoubtedly would have reduced the frequency of deadly snakebites in the social groups of our hominin ancestors," giving them "the evolutionary nudge to begin pointing for social good, a critical step toward the evolution of language."[14]

This drama intensified when our ancestors came down from the treetops and moved their eating game to the expansive savannas, populated by large, ungulate mammals such as cattle and gazelle.[15] Having become omnivorous out of necessity—the savannah was not nearly as plant-rich as the forests had been—these protohuman hunters had to rely on their ability to associate a constellation of sights, smells, and sounds with their prey, time-binding these clues into a discernible trail. "The sequence of signs was itself a path," writes Shepard, "the way evidence gives direction to a mystery."[16]

Some of the most obvious signs on the landscape, both in terms of sight and smell, were the droppings their prey left behind. These "cow pies," as they are euphemistically called, pointed to food at multiple levels: On one level, they indicated where the prey had been and how recently; on another level, they were themselves an easy place to find smaller grub, such as beetles. Modern baboons have been observed flipping over cow pies in Kenya and looking for beetles and other bugs, and there is no reason to believe our early ancestors didn't do the same.[17]

But bugs were not the only food source to be found on cow pies in the African savannah. They were also the preferred growing medium for psilocybin-rich mushrooms such as *Stropharia cubensis*,[18] which would have grown abundantly during the rainy seasons, and which our early ancestors would certainly have noticed and eaten along with the bugs they found while tracking their larger prey. Just like the serpents before them, our ancestral encounters with these novel species would have triggered a series of behavioral and neurological changes over time, changing "the parameters of the process of natural selection," writes ethnobotanist Terrence McKenna, "by changing the behavioral patterns upon which that selection was operating."[19]

These behavioral patterns would have been affected at three different levels, depending on the quantity of mushrooms eaten. In small, nonpsychoactive quantities, psilocybin has been shown to improve vision. If you are trying to track prey from a distance while avoiding venomous snakes in the process, the equivalent of what McKenna calls "chemical binoculars" would have certainly been advantageous.[20]

In slightly larger quantities, the central nervous system activation triggered by these mushrooms would have increased sexual arousal, increasing copulation and reproduction as a result. This would have translated into increased socialization, the tightening of group bonds, and a clear reproductive advantage afforded to those of our ancestors who incorporated these mushrooms into their diet.[21]

In even larger quantities, these mushrooms would have triggered full-blown mystical experiences, in which the mushroom-eater would intuit the communications of the natural world with an otherwise unimaginable subtlety and sophistication. Our archaic human ancestors, then, would have eaten their way into a kind of gnosis—a special knowledge of spiritual mysteries—with the mushroom accelerating the intimate exchange through which early humans developed their sensitivity, awareness, cognition, and pattern-recognizing capabilities.

Summarizing this theory, McKenna writes: "At whatever dose the mushroom was used, it possessed the magical property of conferring adaptive advantages upon its archaic users and their group. Increased visual acuity, sexual arousal, and access to the transcendent Other led to success in obtaining food, sexual prowess and stamina, abundance of offspring, and access to realms of supernatural power."[22]

Unlocking the symbolic and the spiritual would have been greatly accelerated by the visionary psilocybin experience, present in the form of readily available and delicious mushrooms, located conveniently where our ancestors would already have been looking for food. By consuming these mushrooms, our ancestors would have eaten their way out of the punitive world of survival and scarcity and into the world of boundary-dissolution and possibility.

It is here—in the mysterious union of imitation, representation, and linguistic communication—that we can discern the biological origins of our uniquely human mode of perceiving and making sense of the world, a mode that would reach one of its most sophisticated expressions in the forms of visual art and modern science. By projecting intangible elements onto the plants and animals around us, we came to experience the invisible wilderness of the psyche in embodied and sensuous form. As we became more conscious of this power to externalize our inner world, we set the foundations for the emergence of visual art. For the same play-spirit that led us to unlock the invisible world from our physical surroundings eventually led us to represent that world in new, creative forms, such as the hauntingly beautiful cave paintings in Lascaux, France, with images of horses, deer, and other animals believed to be upward of seventeen thousand years old.[23] That these images were understood to correspond to aspects of the human self is revealed by the fact that the only painting of a man in the series is shown with a bird mask over his face—suggesting the interchangeability of the human mind and the world of animal spirits.[24]

In time, we came to express these plant and animal spirits in narrative form, transmitted across the generations as myths and folk tales. As the correspondences between the natural world and these mythic characters became more complex, a constellation of symbols would coalesce around a single, organizing principle—a god—whose multifaceted aspects were each represented by one or another plant or animal.

Many of these myths were then acted out in theater and ritual, such as the divine plays of ancient Greece, with their associated mystery cult initiations. Euripides's famous play *The Bacchae* is a classic example: Centering around the god Dionysus, it debuted at the Dionysia, a large festival in Athens central to the god's mysteries. Throughout the play, the god and his qualities are represented by various plants and animals, such as bulls, bees, ivy, and grape vines. Like the birdman of Lascaux, Dionysus is even considered to be interchangeable with these symbols: When the god, who spent the first half of the play disguised as a human, transforms into his true, divine form, the tragic character Pentheus says: "I see new horns sprouted on your head. Were you ever a wild animal? You're being a bull now."[25]

This same process—through which we projected our inner qualities onto our natural surroundings—abstracted those qualities into unifying principles, and then developed increasingly complex mental frameworks with which to understand those principles and their relation to the natural world, eventually leading to the birth of modern science.

As this process went on, the echoes of its origins in the plant and animal world became increasingly faint. But when we enter playful mystery, we reencounter those origins. For here, science dissolves into a substance indistinguishable from and insolubly bound to the natural world that is its object of study. Perhaps this is why the biologist and animal play researcher Bob Fagen has said that "the study of play encroaches upon spiritual territory, a region where scientists have to confront their own goals and humanity and thus are threatened."[26]

IMAGE AND REALITY OF THE RAVEN

This impulse to explore, imitate, and dream up novel ways of engaging with himself and with the world is what makes the trickster the trickster. Is it any wonder, then, that certain indigenous populations, deeply immersed in and continuously participating with nature, would recognize, and then mythologize, their own creative intelligence, their own wiliness, their own ambiguous relationship with appetite, and their own ambivalence toward the determinism of biological drives in the raven? For all of these qualities, which are contained in that singularly enigmatic word *play*, abound in that animal.

Biologists divide play into three broad types of behavior—locomotor play, object play, and social play—and ravens engage in them all. Locomotor play is characterized by exaggerated or intense movements, such as running, prancing, and leaping, performed for no apparent reason and without any immediate stimulus. Object play involves manipulating, pawing at, pushing, pulling, lifting, carrying, or otherwise messing around with objects in a manner that doesn't appear to provide any immediate benefit, other than being fun.[27] And anytime an animal plays with someone else, it is playing socially.

Ravens often combine multiple types at once, in what the neuroscientist Sergio Pellis calls "superplay." For example, when a raven "hangs upside down by one foot while holding a toy or a piece of wood," then switches "the object from beak to foot and back again," it is engaging in locomotor play and object play at the same time.[28] When a group of ravens "congregate . . . and engage in flight during which pairs roll and tumble and soar together," they are engaging in locomotor and social play at the same time.[29]

Ravens also have a propensity to prioritize their play over their more immediate survival concerns. One study found that "ravens offered the choice of food or play objects most often chose the latter. The object play was so important they could say no to food." Here we find the biological basis for the mythological Raven's impulse to evade the constraints of the survival game. Just as in the myth, these ravens are adept at using play to win that game without being bound by its rules. In *The Bird Way,* Diane Ackerman describes a study in which two researchers constructed "a puzzle-like box containing a high-value treat" and then taught five ravens how to open it using a stone tool. Not only did the ravens quickly learn how to open the box, but when given the choice between eating now or receiving an object that would help them open the box in the future, most of them chose the object play. Some of them even outwitted their experimenters by inventing completely unusual ways to solve the puzzle and get the treat.[30]

Other forms of raven play behavior seem even less obviously related to their biological needs for food or sex. Ravens have often been observed sliding down snow-covered roofs on their backs, only to quickly return to the tops of the inclines and slide again. In one particularly amusing incident, an observer reported seeing large groups of ravens sliding down a muddy incline along the high banks of a river, vocalizing loudly as if they were laughing. "This noise was heard over a mile before we paddled up to the birds, where we stopped to witness their amusement," he writes. "The trees in the vicinity contained numbers of ravens aiding the sport with their cries of approval or taking their turns as the others became tired."[31] Summarizing a selection of similar findings, Henrich and Smolker concluded simply that they saw "no obvious utilitarian benefit" for this behavior.[32]

THE HOBGOBLIN OF ANIMAL BEHAVIOR

I begin with the raven, and the ambiguous relationship between its survival needs and its play, because this ambiguity strikes at the heart of the problems concerning the discussion of play in a biological context, or with scientific specificity. To explore these problems, let's again ask ourselves: What is play? Why does it occur? What functions does it serve? Where is the boundary across which life stops being playful and starts being serious? And how can we talk about that boundary in a scientific context, in which statements like "I know it when I see it" are insufficiently precise?

Biologists tend to characterize animal play as both "adaptive" and "apparently purposeless" at the same time.[33] Play must be adaptive, they argue, or else it would not have emerged or persisted in an evolutionary context. Stuart Brown speaks to this when he points out that "mountain goats bound playfully along rock faces thousands of feet high, and sometimes they fall . . . over time, if play had no benefit, the playful goats would be pushed out of the gene pool by the offspring of the nonplayers. But that is not what happens, so there must be some advantage." Bob and Joanna Fagen provide further support for this criteria by ending their ten-year study of play behavior among Alaskan bears with the conclusion that "the bears that played the most were the ones who survived the best . . . despite the fact that playing takes away time, attention, and energy from activities like eating, which seem at first glance to contribute more to the bears' survival."[34]

Play must also be purposeless, they argue, or else it would not be play, but some other serious behavior. Here we encounter the strongest evidence of the serious myth's influence upon the scientific discourse on play—an influence that Fagen himself pushes back against by qualifying his own play definition with the caveat that it is ultimately "a matter of taste whether behaviors that do not . . . satisfy the criteria . . . are to be called *play*."[35] For the moment that a behavior can be ascribed to some other concern, the more reductive scientist will cease to call it play and instead claim triumphantly to have discovered its *true* (that is, serious) function. In this antiquated view, nature is seen as all "tooth and claw,"[36] as mostly serious, and only under certain narrow conditions playful.

But what if it is the observing scientist, and not the observed world, that is the *mostly serious* entity? Is it not possible, asks Feyerabend, that a "theory may be inconsistent with the evidence, not because it is incorrect, but because the evidence is contaminated," in this case by the taken-for-granted assumptions of a serious worldview that treats life as burdensome and nature as punitive? Here again we come across the treatment of play as "not work" in a division that takes teleology for granted.

Biologist and animal play expert Marc Bekoff skirts this division by concluding that animals play "for the fun of it," and that this fun is itself the purpose of their activity.[37] In other words, animal play is autotelic. Though there may be secondary benefits that arise—either immediately or at some point further down the line—the joy of the play is primary and not reducible to those benefits.

For why—if the elderly women of the European Alps can approach their manual labor with a playful orientation—would there not be evolutionary antecedents for such an approach to behavior? Is it not possible that the bird of paradise *enjoys* its courtship dance? Or that sex, for the animals just as for us, can be both adaptive *and* fun? What would happen to our scientific worldview if we expanded our definition of play to include even this kind of immediately adaptive behavior, even when survival and procreation are on the line?

SINGING FOR THE FUN OF IT

The singing of birds is just one such activity. The behaviorist view is to reduce the bird's singing to its survival needs, specifically its need to attract a mate and defend its territory. But to say that a bird's singing increases its likelihood of mating or defending its territory is to say nothing of what it *feels* like, subjectively, for the bird to sing. Inverting the typical logic, which says something like, "if birds enjoy their singing, that is because this hardwired enjoyment increases their likelihood of reproduction." Birdwatcher and theologian Charles Hartshorne suggests that birds might reproduce *because they enjoy their singing and want more song in the world.* In another inversion, he suggests that territorial songbirds might sing *because they like their territory* and therefore *want to keep it.* In both cases, aesthetic enjoyment is the primary motivation of the bird's singing behavior.[38]

The moment we speculate about the inner experience of a nonhuman animal, we risk accusations of anthropomorphism. But, as Hartshorne points out, the behaviorist is no less anthropomorphic when they hear, in the singing of a songbird, the message: "get away or I'll peck your eyes out!"[39] Hartshorne views the natural world in a third way—not just as a scientist, or a theologian, but somehow neither and both at once.

One could argue that bees, being insects after all, are incapable of play behavior. But in fact, there is ample evidence that bees do play. Juvenile honeybees, for example, have been observed climbing to the top of their hive, jumping off, flapping their wings, floating to the ground, and climbing up to do it again.[40]

Bees might also play with the flowers that attract them—the flowers toward which they fly. Would a flower's aesthetic beauty be a consideration in the bee's selection process, if they didn't enjoy beauty and want to see more of it in the world? It seems only natural that the dance between the flowers and the bees is a form of erotic play.

Any aversion to this interpretation has less to do with science as such and more to do with the scientist's criteria for what science can be. When the scientist looks out into the world of vibrant color and exquisite song and sees only the mechanics of sexual reproduction and antagonistic violence, this says more about the scientist's own relationship to beauty and sexuality than it does about the bird's or the bee's.

MAXIMIZING UNEXPECTEDNESS

Many bird species sing best long after their mating season has ended and when their territory is not under threat. To reduce birdsong to mating and territorial needs, then, is to leave a large quantity of song unexplained. As for the structural content: Hartshorne has observed that even birds with biologically fixed songs still vary the lengths of the pauses between their performances of those songs, to avoid repetition. "What seems to stimulate the singing is change, and what deadens it is sameness or persistent repetition." Hartshorne's conclusion, then, is that the aim of birdsong is not to maximize reproduction, but to "maximize unexpectedness."[41]

This insertion of a personal sense of aesthetic timing into an otherwise rigidly hardwired behavior characterizes the creativity of the bird and its vocal play. "The musical sense of the bird is biologically useful," writes philosopher Daniel Dombrowski, "but to admit this much is not necessarily to claim that the bird cannot enjoy . . . its partially unpredictable song . . . Aesthetic value, as opposed to religious value, is thus not peculiar to our species."[42]

Biologists have hypothesized the existence of a birdsong template in which different species are "wired to learn some kinds of songs rather than others."[43] This model accounts for the predisposition of certain birds to learn certain songs at the species level, while still leaving enough space for creative freedom at the individual level.

Although the ability to sing may be instinctive, the actual songs themselves are learned. This learning process is characterized by the pleasure of imitation. "One sign of pleasure in patterns of sound is the tendency to imitate them," writes Hartshorne. "That there is a good deal of this in bird life we know, since it has been established that in many species, hearing adults of the species sing helps the young to learn the proper songs."[44]

Here we find a parallel to the pleasure that we ourselves derive from imitation. Just as humans mythologized their own playfulness by seeing in the raven an outward and visible expression of an inward mystery, so too does the young songbird imitate its elder's melody, and derive some pleasure in doing so, because it hears in that song an outward expression of inner, aesthetic potential—a concrete manifestation of an unformed creative urge.

RAVEN GAMES AND THE PURSUIT OF MASTERY

This unfolding of creative expression can be distilled down to two fundamental behaviors: imitation and elaboration. Fueled by the convergence of aesthetic impulse and evolutionary pressure, the bird's imitation allows him to live out and express an inner urge creatively, to internalize and then act out something perceived in the other—be it an alluring melody, a well-proportioned nest, or some other work of beauty. From there, their only concern is to see how far they can push the song, the craft, the play. This is not a projection of human self-consciousness onto the birds; it is simply a description of the way that adaptive behaviors are fueled, and are themselves infused with beauty, novelty, and complexity.

This impulse to continually push the edge is the heart of self-assessment theory, which biologist Katerina Thompson suggests "may provide a framework for the speculative link between play and creativity."[45] The theory states that, as an individual animal becomes increasingly competent at a given challenge, it will generate more difficult challenges in order to continually test itself. These challenges will typically involve some element of uncertainty, unfamiliarity, and risk. To assess and mitigate the severity of this risk, a feedback loop of increasing reliability is cultivated between the animal, its playmates, and its environment. "The more well-rounded the feedback," writes Thompson, "the more informed the decision" to play.[46]

Many of the characteristics of a well-constructed game are accounted for by this framework. Although games may assume their most elaborate forms in human play, there is plenty of evidence that other species enjoy a good game as much as we do. One biologist, for example, observed a group of ravens playing in the wind on some loose power lines: "The wires were about a foot apart and flailing sinuously in the strong wind. First one raven would try to land on the lower wire and as it moved up and down, try to grab the upper wire in its beak. Once, one of them grabbed it with its foot instead and hung on as it whipsawed up and down in the wind. It looked like the goal was simply to hang on for as long as possible, a sort of raven rodeo. As soon as the first raven was tossed off or lost its grip . . . the next raven would attempt the same feat."[47] All of the elements of Thompson's self-assessment theory are present in this raven game: a group of ravens in a novel situation freely choose to risk a challenging behavior, and rely on the observation of their friends as feedback for what's possible and where the edge is— for what to imitate and where to elaborate.

But biologists qualify these reports by saying that even behavior that appears playful to us may in fact be serious to the ravens. "Because ravens generally mate monogamously and for life," write Heinrich and Smolker, "successful competition in the mate-choice arena is absolutely critical to lifetime reproduction."[48] Much of the behavior that we consider to be free play, such as "flight acrobatics, hanging upside down, dropping and catching objects in flight," and so on, may therefore actually be attempts to signal sexual fitness to potential mates.[49]

The assumption is that any behavior with an immediately adaptive function can no longer be regarded as play. But, to say that a playful behavior has reproductive consequences is to say nothing about how ravens experience their play. Consider the human parallel, where an athlete or a musician can both enjoy their play *and* increase their sexual opportunities because of their skillfulness. Why would such an overlap between enjoyment, skilled play, and reproductive fitness not also exist for other animals? Shepard speaks to this possibility when he points out that "the game of mateship, like the ecological intercourse of predator and prey, has reciprocal customs and stratagems," and concludes that "mateship and cultural facilitation of courting are both play in its larger sense."[50]

You could argue that courtship behavior is too high-stakes, and so too stressful to be enjoyable. Burghardt, for example, includes as one of his criteria for play that "the behavior is initiated when the animal is . . . free from stress . . . or intense competing systems (e.g., feeding, mating, predator avoidance)."[51] But elsewhere he acknowledges that, "in our own species, at least, play can itself become stressful as the social competition or difficulty of the game becomes frustrating. Thus we can view play plus stress as fostering creativity by rewarding novel ways of solving some challenge."[52]

The line between play and nonplay is ambiguous, and the raven, as trickster, is the embodiment of this ambiguity. He is the one who plays with the categories of hunter and hunted, the one who adapts by playing with the criteria for adaptation itself. He is the one who takes the stress of survival into the boundaries of his play, seeing what he can do with it. He is the one with the freedom to step outside of the survival game and critique it, only to step back into that game and outperform the others as a result of his expanded perspective.

When his archetype expresses itself in the play behavior of animals, it subverts not only *biology* but *biologists*: For anything measured can be controlled; and play refuses to be controlled. A playful science, then, must be willing to let go and allow itself to be continually surprised. It must adopt a sense of curiosity and openness akin to that of the child, for whom everything is new and awe-inspiring.

MAPPING THE PLAYGROUND

When the archetypal trickster assumes human form in his mythology, he is almost always represented as a divine child. There are good biological reasons for this. Especially for species with extended parental care, childhood provides the safety and containment to freely explore and learn about the world in a low-stakes context. If an individual is being fed by its mother and is too young to worry about mating pressures, then it is free to experiment, discover novel forms of engagement, and make sense of itself and its capabilities in the process. Put another way, a young and cared for animal can play with play, without having to learn the more complex task of playing with survival.

Play researcher John Byers has found that "the period of maximum play in each species is tied to the rate and size of growth of the cerebellum," a region involved in motor control and coordination, as well as a host of other specialized functions like language processing and attention control.[53] For most species, this period occurs during youth. Consider how a young raven might make sense of its body—how it orients in space and what it is capable of doing—as it swings upside down from a loose wire. Or how a young, play-fighting bear might learn the rules and limits of social engagement, the subtle cues of others, and the emotional states they signify, by wrestling with their friends.

In the language of child psychologist Jean Piaget, the playfulness of youth allows infants to "assimilate information from their environment (including their own bodies) and accommodate their cognitive apparatus to it and thus proceed through the stages of cognitive development."[54]

Stuart Brown has proposed a framework for how this might happen, based on the Nobel laureate and neuroscientist Gerald Edelman's work on information processing. According to Edelman's theory, our brains encode our sensory experiences into cognitive maps, which consist of complex and interconnected neural networks. For example, the wide variety of dog breeds—from squishy-nosed Pugs to imposing German Shepherds—are all encoded into a single map for "dogness," allowing us to quickly recognize dogs we've never seen before and assimilate them into a larger, preexisting category. "In this way the brain achieves a rich and flexible series of maps that permit the recognition of innumerable sorts of objects, sounds, colors, social settings, and so on," writes Brown. "The perceptual generalizations arising from these maps are not static. They flex and change. They also have emotional connotations. We find our way in the world by navigating this huge and organically growing cartography of life."[55]

Brown's major contribution to Edelman's theory is the idea that these maps increase in their depth, flexibility, and dynamism—their "vitality," to use his word—most rapidly through play.[56] This is because the exploratory engagement with and curious orientation toward play provides us with the freedom to try out new patterns of behavior. In play, we discover new things we can do with objects, and new responses we can elicit from others. As a result, our maps become more detailed and sophisticated. Our image of the world retains its plasticity and flexibility—and so do our minds.

Any animal capable of envisioning potential strategies and anticipating possible outcomes because of these increasingly sophisticated neural maps would have an advantage over those around them that were unable to do so. "Play can thus be involved in creativity and behavioral innovation," writes Burghardt, "not just in the choice of different behavioral options, but through selection for animals that can create such options via internal processes."[57] These internal processes, which assume their richest form in the human imagination, allow us to withdraw ourselves temporarily from the unconscious instinct to act on our biological imperatives. We can exit the survival game, at least for a moment, and play with our options—even inventing new ones.

Through play, that is, we both construct a map of what already is and dream into being a map of what could be. It is this leap from the rudimentary, object-oriented, exploratory behavior through which the animal in us maps the world as it is, to the intuitive perception and inward rendering of the world as it could be, that constitutes the first influx of imagination, in however inchoate a form.

One day, in October 1913, while riding a train to the Swiss town of Schaffhausen, the Swiss psychiatrist Carl Jung had a disturbing vision in which he saw Europe being destroyed by a catastrophic flood. "I was traveling by train and had a book in my hand that I was reading," he later recalled. "I began to fantasize and before I knew it . . . I was looking down on the map of Europe in relief. I saw all the northern part, and England sinking down so that the sea came in upon it. . . . I realized that a frightful catastrophe was in progress. . . . At first I was only looking dispassionately, and then the sense of the catastrophe gripped me with tremendous power."[58]

When the vision reoccurred two weeks later and was accompanied by catastrophic dreams, Jung began to fear for his sanity. To get a grip on his reality, he began to build sandcastles on the shore of Lake Zurich, just as he had done as a child. "As soon as I was through eating, I began playing," he writes in his memoir, "and continued to do so until the patients arrived; and if I was finished with my work early enough in the evening, I went back to the building. In the course of this activity my thoughts clarified, and I was able to grasp the fantasies whose presence in myself I dimly felt."[59]

Eventually, Jung moved from physically digging holes in the ground to visualizing himself digging holes in his imagination. By descending into the depths of his psyche this way, Jung uncovered and integrated the catastrophic images that had been haunting him. "In order to grasp the fantasies which were stirring in me 'underground,'" he writes, "I knew that I had to let myself plummet down into them."[60]

The visionary landscape of this imaginary world, as well as the bizarre and dreamlike figures that he encountered there, shocked and bewildered him. The thought of conversing with a set of imaginary friends only escalated his fear of losing touch with reality. But "after prolonged hesitation, I saw that there was no other way out. I had to take the chance, had to try to gain power over [my fantasies]; for I realized that if I did not do so, I ran the risk of their gaining power over me. A cogent motive for my making the attempt was the conviction that I could not expect of my patients something I did not dare to do myself."[61]

Jung then faithfully transcribed every one of these imaginal encounters into a large, red, leather-bound book. He wrote in a calligraphic style, illuminating the pages with images from his visions in the manner of a medieval manuscript. In doing so, he gave creative form to the primal images that were stirring in the depths of his soul, binding them into a tangible, concrete work of arresting beauty and wisdom.

Yet, for the serious, scientifically trained psychiatrist in him, this all struck him as absurd, distasteful, and a further sign of his waning sanity. As he later told the religious scholar Mircea Eliade: "As a psychiatrist I became worried, wondering if I was not on the way to 'doing a schizophrenia,' as we said in the language of those days. . . . I was just preparing a lecture on schizophrenia to be delivered at a congress in Aberdeen, and I kept saying to myself: 'I'll be speaking of myself! I'll very likely go mad after reading out this paper' . . . [but] on July 31st, immediately after my lecture, I learned from the newspapers that war had broken out. Finally I understood. And when I disembarked in Holland on the next day, nobody was happier than I. Now I was sure that no schizophrenia was threatening me. I understood that my dreams and my visions came to me from the subsoil of the collective unconscious. What remained for me to do now was to deepen and validate this discovery. And this is what I have been trying to do for forty years."[62]

By engaging with his dreams and visions through the free play of his creative imagination, Jung distilled and extracted the meaning of these experiences and their relevance to global affairs and human psychology. This distillation was achieved, not through rational analysis, but through a return to the sand play and fantasizing of his childhood. By following the natural course of this child's play, Jung paradoxically arrived at his most mature and enduring insights. For as he later writes, the years "when I pursued the inner images, were the most important time of my life. Everything else is to be derived from this . . . everything later was merely the outer classification, the scientific elaboration, and the integration into life. But the numinous beginning, which contained everything, was then."[63]

THE COYOTE, THE WOLF, AND THE FOUNTAIN OF YOUTH

To further unravel the mysterious threads linking youth, flexibility, and adaptation with animal play and human imagination, let's turn from the Raven to the Coyote, another representative of the trickster archetype.

The following fragment of a Nez Perce tale is representative:

Coyote and Fox were wandering. They were hungry. Coyote said: "I am too lazy to hunt for myself. Let somebody else provide food for me."

"You mean for *us*," said Fox.

"Well, all right, for us."

"How do we do this?" Fox asked.

"You take after your father," said Coyote. "He was slow-witted, and so are you. I take after my father, who was wise; therefore I am very clever. Let us marry some men who are good hunters and will provide for us."

"How can we marry men when we ourselves are men?"

"We will disguise ourselves by putting on women's clothes. They won't know that we are men."[64]

Coyote and Fox then cross-dress as women, travel to the Wolf brothers' lodge, and tell them that their parents had arranged for them to be married. The wolves, successfully duped, agree to the arrangement and insist on cohabiting immediately. But Coyote, expecting this, has other plans:

"Not so fast," said Coyote, "Before we marry and sleep with you, we must make sure that you can provide for beautiful maidens such as us. For four days you shall feed us—only the best, mind you. Then, after we have satisfied ourselves that you are skilled hunters, we will marry and cohabit."[65]

The wolves accept Coyote's offer. And, after four days of leisurely eating, Coyote uses another trick to distract the brothers long enough for him and Fox to make their escape.

THE COYOTE'S COMMENTARY

Here, the Coyote, like the Raven, manages to satisfy his appetite while standing outside of the hunter-and-hunted game. As with the Tlingit authors of the Raven tale, the Nez Perce had good reasons to render their trickster as a coyote. For, as Hyde has shown, the folklore of the early American West is replete with tales of coyotes behaving playfully. Early sheep farmers had tried to clear out the local coyote and wolf populations near their farms by leaving out carcasses poisoned with strychnine. The trick successfully killed large numbers of wolves, but the coyotes caught on quickly and avoided the bait.[66]

When early hunters set out metal leg traps to catch coyotes, the animals were rarely fooled. Often, they responded with a message of their own. "It is difficult to escape the conclusion that coyotes . . . have a sense of humor," writes Hyde, quoting a naturalist. "How else to explain, for instance, the well-known propensity of experienced coyotes to dig up traps, turn them over, and urinate or defecate on them?" Here, the coyote subverts the context of the hunting game, overturning its instruments and undermining its seriousness with his distinctive sense of humor. "And what trapper's pride could remain unshaken," writes Hyde, "once he's read Coyote's commentary?"[67]

This brings us to another significant detail in the story, namely the contrast between the Coyote's cunning and the Wolf's gullibility. It is no coincidence that the Nez Perce chose the wolf as the Coyote's victim: For wild coyotes demonstrate a great plasticity of behavior not seen in wolves. They prolong characteristics of their youth long into adulthood, in what biologists call neoteny. "Since early development is a time when the nervous system is most 'plastic,'" writes Brown, "an advantage that neoteny bestows is extended openness to change, and sustained curiosity, as well as the ability to readily incorporate new information."[68]

To illustrate this distinction, let's contrast the developmental biology of wolves with that of dogs—a species both more familiar to us and more closely related to them. When wolves and dogs are puppies, they look and behave very similarly: They both have floppy ears and short, squishy muzzles, and they both love to play. If you throw a stick or a bone for a wolf pup, it will run and retrieve it for you just as eagerly and playfully as a Labrador will. The difference is that the Labrador will retain these characteristics all the way into old age. But, for the wolf pup, this playful behavior and juvenile physiology will only be a developmental step on the way to adulthood.[69]

In time, the wolf's physical features will change—the nose will elongate and become pointed, and the ears will stand sharply upright—and behavior will change as well. The wolf will begin to devote more time and energy toward establishing a fixed, hierarchical position in the wolf pack and functioning cohesively within that pack order as a group hunter. Though this will allow the wolf to hunt very effectively, there will be trade-offs associated with this effectiveness: Wolves "will inevitably remain bound by narrower and more compulsive behaviors than a domestic dog."[70]

But coyotes, like dogs, are a highly neotenous species, and this neoteny, the retention of juvenile characteristics in adults, has allowed them to flexibly adapt to changing environmental conditions in ways that wolves could not. As the naturalist François Leydet points out, coyotes of the early American West were social hunters, just like wolves. But, these days, "big gatherings of coyotes are seldom seen . . . persecution forced coyotes to adopt more solitary ways, and since they subsist largely on small game that they can catch unassisted, they have been able to do so. This has allowed them to survive in regions where the big gray wolf has been exterminated: A hunter of large game, *Canis lupus* would not or could not abandon the pack organization, which made him highly vulnerable to man."[71]

For when it comes to neoteny, there is one species that outdoes them all: our own. We humans are the great imitators of the natural world. And the whole scientific enterprise, along with mythology, philosophy, art, theater, ritual, and so much else that makes us uniquely human, is borne of our extended juvenile period. "It is human to have a long childhood," writes psychiatrist Erik Erikson, and "it is civilized to have an even longer childhood. Long childhood makes a technical and mental virtuoso out of man."[72]

By suspending some or all of our immediate survival needs for the first couple decades of life, civilization affords us the freedom to pursue higher-complexity intellectual and creative tasks. Our entire school system, when it is functioning properly, is meant to facilitate this process. From the negotiation of roles and sharing of toys on the preschool playground; to the study of world literature, chemistry, and calculus in high school; and even to the learning of ancient languages, arcane theorems, or classical concertos in college and graduate school, civilization harnesses the neoteny of our species to cultivate skills of increasing sophistication for the advancement of our society.

MORE THAN ANY OTHER SPECIES, the expression of this neoteny is ultimately up to us as individuals: We can decide to become rigid as adults, conform to our society, and constrict our range of creative play. But, just as freely, we can dissolve those boundaries. We can update our cognitive maps, keeping them flexible enough to receive new ideas and stay open to innovation.

Stuart Brown calls humans "the Labradors of the primate world" for this reason. "Just as Labrador and wolf pups look and act alike," he writes, "chimpanzee babies look very much like human babies, with high, rounded foreheads and big eyes." But we retain these physical features throughout our lives, whereas chimps undergo a series of physiological changes as they approach maturity. Just as with wolves, these physiological changes coincide with increased social and behavioral rigidity. As male chimpanzees mature, they enter into fixed dominance hierarchies and react violently toward strangers—especially those that encroach upon their territory. "They seem to like to fight more than play," writes Brown, and there are neurological consequences to this rigidity: a damaged, adult chimpanzee nervous system has less capacity for repair than a human's, which is much more capable of regenerating itself—"a characteristic of being forever young."[73]

The discovery of this neuroplasticity has completely overturned the old view of the nervous system as largely inflexible. "The common wisdom was that after childhood the brain changed only when it began the long process of decline," writes psychiatrist Norman Doidge, "that when brain cells failed to develop properly, or were injured, or died, they could not be replaced."[74]

But this is no longer the case, thanks to the work of pioneering neuroscientists like Paul Bach-y-Rita. In his book *The Brain That Changes Itself,* Doidge tells us how Bach-y-Rita came to see the human nervous system as significantly more malleable than was previously believed.

It all started when Paul's father, Pedro, a poet and college professor, suffered a debilitating stroke that paralyzed much of his body and left him unable to speak.[75] After Pedro's doctors told the family that he would never recover and would need to be institutionalized, Paul's brother, George, decided to move Pedro from New York to Mexico to live with him instead.

"George knew nothing about rehabilitation," writes Doidge, "and his ignorance turned out to be a godsend, because he succeeded by breaking all its current rules, unencumbered by pessimistic theories."[76]

His method involved having Pedro crawl around on the floor and play simple games, learning step by step how to move and speak just as he did when he was a child. "The only model I had was how babies learn," George recalls. "So we played games on the floor, with me rolling marbles and him having to catch them. Or we'd throw coins on the floor, and he'd have to try and pick them up with his weak right hand. . . . There were steps, each one overlapping with the one before, and little by little he got better. After a while he helped to design the steps. He wanted to get to the point where he could sit down and eat with me and the other medical students."[77]

The strategy worked. By reconnecting Pedro to the power of child's play, George helped him leverage the neotenous quality of the human nervous system to regenerate itself. In time, Pedro "went from crawling, to moving on his knees, to standing, to walking." He then gradually learned to write again, regained his ability to speak, and went back to teaching at the City College in New York.[78] After seven more years of teaching, traveling, and working, Pedro had a heart attack at nine-thousand-feet elevation, during a hike in Bogotá, Colombia, with his friends. He died soon afterward, at the age of seventy-two.

Remarkably, his autopsy revealed the presence of extreme brain damage, including in regions that control movement, which had never healed from the stroke. "I knew that meant that somehow his brain had totally reorganized itself with the work he did with George," Paul writes. In other words, by tapping into the innate playfulness of his biology, Pedro completely rewired his nervous system, allowing it to reconfigure its elements in a kind of neural bricolage, through which the healthy parts of his brain began to take on the functions previously performed by the damaged parts. This kind of recovery could only occur in a species as neotenous as ours, a species in which a return to a childlike state of openness and flexibility is possible at any age.

THE VULNERABILITY OF CONTACT

The fact that less neotenous species like chimpanzees "like to fight more than play" leaves us with another question: What happens when fighting itself becomes a form of play? What exactly is going on when animals play fight?

Early research on the subject noted the structural similarity of play fighting to other serious behaviors like hunting, and concluded that the play behavior might be a way to practice that serious behavior. But more recent research has shown that animals that have been experimentally deprived of the opportunity to play still manage to hunt just fine. They don't, however, learn to socialize properly. "Cats and other social mammals such as rats will, if seriously missing out on play, have an inability to clearly delineate friend from foe," writes Brown. They will "miscue on social signaling, and either act excessively aggressive or retreat and not engage in more normal social patterns."[79] Play-fighting allows these animals to learn the rules of engagement with others; when a young animal is deprived of this opportunity, its social and emotional intelligence will atrophy.

THIS EMOTIONAL ATROPHY leaves a neurological fingerprint. "Laboratory rats deprived of play don't develop normal brains," writes Ackerman. "Scientists discovered this by housing juvenile rats with adults, which inhibits their play impulses. The young rats, which had all of the other kinds of social interaction—touching, sniffing, and so on, but no play, did not develop a normal prefrontal cortex."[80] The same applies to nonmammals, such as birds. Sergio Pellis's research has shown that "play changes the social brain. Playing with others modifies the connections between neurons in the prefrontal cortex, and these changes likely mediate the development of social competence in any animal. Birds deprived of play in youth will not play into adulthood—and may struggle to fit into social groupings."[81]

It turns out that we humans experience the same social and developmental issues when deprived of play, especially during childhood. A tragic example of this is the case of Charles Whitman, an architectural engineering student at the University of Texas, Austin, who climbed a campus tower in August 1966 and began shooting at the people below at random. An ex-marine, Whitman fired with devastating accuracy,

killing fifteen and wounding thirty-one before an off-duty police offi-
cer and an armed civilian gunned him down.[82]

Stuart Brown, who was part of the committee of toxicologists, neu-
rologists, psychologists, and other experts gathered to assess how this
tragedy could have happened, recalls that everyone on the committee
had initially expected the shooter to be a "ravingly paranoid maniac."
So they were astonished to discover that he was, by all accounts, a loving husband and son.[83]

Looking deeper into Whitman's history, they began to get a clearer
picture of what could have driven him to such a senseless act. Charles
had an extremely controlling and overbearing father, who abused both
him and his mother all throughout his childhood. This was certainly a
critical factor. "But the incredibly thorough investigation of Charlie's
whole life revealed a more surprising factor," writes Brown. While some
researchers have speculated that neurologic injury and "a fascination
with guns as early as age two contributed to his later violent turn," after
extensive interviews with everyone who had entered Charlie's life, it
became clear that *the lifelong lack of play* had itself been an important
factor in his psychopathology."[84]

The committee determined that, "at many junctures in Charlie's life,
he could not see outside the box that his father had placed him in. The
multiple options found in a free-flowing imagination, which occur
spontaneously in a naturally playful, safely nurtured child, were not
available. The open exchanges that begin in preschool parallel play, the
broadening spectrum of give-and-take offered in pickup games, and the
variety of choices that more intricate play provides were not his to
experience."[85]

Neuroscientist Jaak Panksepp's work on the developmental role
of play fighting in mammals has found that "abundant access to
rough-and-tumble play" can reduce "the impulsivity of rats with frontal lobe damage," leading him "and his colleagues [to] propose that a

regimen of social, boisterous play might be one way to help children with mild to moderate ADHD control impulsivity."[86] In other words, contrary to the helicopter-parent model, play-fighting, when undertaken within a context of trust, safety, and moderation, can actually reduce violence among children and adults by giving them a chance to develop the social and neurological structures to handle ambiguity, read social cues, and respond flexibly under pressure.

Still, of all the forms of social play, play fighting is undoubtedly the most intimate and vulnerable. Because "play fighting is by definition a contact activity," writes animal play expert Maxeen Biben, "and close contact with strangers or those whose intentions are unclear is . . . [a] stressor."[87] Any animal with the desire to play, then, must be able to effectively communicate its intentions to potential playmates—letting them know that they are just playing and not really fighting. Because any miscommunication, any misinterpretation of their behavior, could inadvertently result in actual combat.

In the case of bears, cats, and other animals with sharp teeth and claws, actual combat could mean serious injury or even death. So, these animals have developed sophisticated methods of signaling their intention to play. For example, when two dogs meet and then assume a bowing posture—known as the "play bow"—they are communicating to each other that "what follows is play, regardless of how aggressive it may appear." The philosopher Gregory Bateson calls these *metacommunications*: behaviors that signal what the following behaviors mean.[88] The metacommunication signals to the playmate that it is safe to relax their vigilance, that "this is play." They feel safe enough to let their guard down and improvise. They can test their limits and expand their repertoire of physical and social behaviors in the process. Most important, they can have fun.

Other animals have devised their own metacommunications for play, based on how they navigate the world. Rodents, for example, are less visual and more olfactory, and communicate their play signals through "distinctive odors" known as "play pheromones." Mongooses communicate their play signals vocally, emitting "a whistle only heard during social play." Squirrel monkeys accompany their play fights with cackles, performed much louder than necessary for their partners to hear them. Burghardt speculates that the purpose of these cackles might be to "inform nearby adults . . . that the interactions are playful." In this case, the signal may mean something like, "Don't worry, we are just playing."[89]

An amusing play signal is the warble sound that keas make during their play. As part of his PhD research, the biologist Raoul Schwing set up speakers in a wild kea habitat and recorded the birds' reactions to various sounds. When he played the warble sound, the birds suddenly looked at each other, "burst into squeals, and [launched] into play, becoming exceedingly silly, chasing each other, flapping up and down, picking up rocks and flinging them," among other play behaviors. Schwing documented a 500 percent increase (!) in play behavior in response to the warble sound. He also found that everyone joined in on these spontaneous eruptions of play, not only juveniles but also adults, including members of the opposite sex. In this case, the metacommunication might mean something like: "playtime!"[90]

Scientists have yet to determine why keas would have developed a play signal directed simultaneously toward so many playmates. But Schwing speculates that it may have something to do with keas' unique social organization. Most communities of social animals organize themselves into dominance hierarchies, in which status is secured through fighting. But keas don't do that. "In four years of fieldwork in New Zealand, I never saw two adult kea fight," he says. "Not once." They may not even have dominance hierarchies at all. "If you go to what I call a hot spot in the mountains, where you have conglomerations of thirty kea, they mingle in very fluid groups," he says. "You might have two birds arrive, then six, then three birds fly away, five birds come in, four birds fly away . . . we're talking hourly changeover of maybe half the group. If the kea had a true hierarchy, they would be fighting all the time." Instead, they seem to dissipate their social tension through play: they wrestle, chase each other, throw things, and goof around, "as a social facilitator," which "obviates the need for a hierarchy based on fighting." Perhaps this is why the locals call them the "clowns of the mountains."[91] Keas are always reminding each other, and those who spend time around them, to not take things too seriously.

ROLE REVERSAL

But what about those animals that *do* organize themselves into fixed dominance hierarchies? How does a dominant animal engage in play-fighting without undermining its hard-earned status in the hierarchy?

Here, again, play signals go a long way: By communicating to their play partner and those around them that "what follows is play," the more dominant animal can be sure that everyone knows they are not actually fighting. This gives them the freedom to not have to dominate their opponent, as nothing serious is on the line. It also gives them the chance to attract a willing play partner. Because it is not enough for a dominant animal to want to play with a subordinate animal; they also need that animal to want to play with them. And it turns out that animals, just like us, only want to play when they have a reasonable chance of winning at least some of the time. Studies have shown, for example, that rhesus macaques will not continue to play unless both players have a somewhat equal chance of winning.[92]

To secure a playmate, then, the bigger, stronger animal will engage in behavior that biologists call self-handicapping. This involves using "less advantageous strategies, [inhibiting] his or her behavior, or otherwise [acting] to keep the 'opponent' in the game."[93] The beauty of self-handicapping is that it allows players to periodically switch roles—with the typically dominant player assuming a submissive position and the typically submissive player assuming a dominant position. Because this role-reversal occurs in the context of play, the dominant player can rest assured that their position in the hierarchy is not under threat.

Maxeen Biben has gone so far as to suggest that this inversion of roles might be one of the main purposes of play fighting itself, and not merely a way to secure a playmate. By assuming a subordinate position, a normally dominant monkey could practice keeping his cool in a high-stress situation. "When a juvenile male gives up, in play, opportunities to be dominant, he may gain experience in both the motor and cognitive aspects of being subordinate," she writes, "and because dominance roles during and outside of play are separate, he can do so without abdicating his normally dominant role."[94] Should he find himself in a subordinate position in a serious fight later on, he will be able to rely on his play-fighting experience to stay relaxed and flexible in an otherwise threatening circumstance.

Ackerman corroborates this hypothesis when she points out that "some kinds of play fighting . . . include elements of real fighting and activate the same neurochemical pathways in . . . [the] brain as the fight-or-flight response. By creating little peaks of mild stress in safe circumstances, play fighting might alter . . . [an animal's] sensitivity to stress, so the next time [they] encounter a truly stressful challenge, it's not as traumatized and recovers more quickly."[95] Play fighting, then, both softens otherwise rigid social hierarchies and reduces traumatic stress responses by giving animals the opportunity to expose themselves vulnerably in a low-stakes environment.

This same method of self-handicapping lies at the foundation of coach John Danaher's approach to teaching jiujitsu. Widely believed to be among the best coaches in the history of the sport, Danaher says that he's "a huge advocate of handicap training, where you handicap to work on skills."[96] By having his more dominant students assume subordinate positions, he instills in them the confidence to remain cool under pressure, as well as the physical skills to escape those positions and ultimately win the fight.

"You can train someone and teach them technique until you're blue in the face," he says, "but at some point the athlete in question has to go out there on the stage and pull the trigger when the time is right. What's gonna give you that ability to go from the physical skills that you've learned to execution under pressure is confidence," and this confidence stems directly from the knowledge that you can continue to fight even if you find yourself in a bad position.

By allowing your training partners to assume dominant positions in the low-stakes activity of practice sparring, you "take away the innate fear that we all have of bad outcomes that makes us naturally risk averse. When you don't believe you can be pinned . . . you'll take risks, because there's no downside to your actions. . . . Building that confidence is the key to championship performance."[97]

THE ULTIMATE PARADOX

At the end of the day, when all other functional or adaptive explanations fall away, play still endures—simply because it's fun. Stuart Brown proves as much when he recounts the following play fight between a sled dog and a wild bear: After approaching each other with a series of play signals such as curvilinear movement rather than direct sprinting; open mouths with concealed teeth; flattened hair; and gentle eye contact, the two "wrestled and rolled around so energetically that at one point the bear had to lie down, belly up: a universal sign in the animal kingdom for a time-out. At another point during their romp, the bear paused to envelop [the dog] in an affectionate embrace."[98]

Here, play ventures much further than the boundaries between dominant and submissive peers, overcoming even the boundaries between species. It does so not because it's adaptive, not because it increases neurological flexibility or social intelligence, but simply because it's fun. It's fun to set aside the survival game and roll around in the snow with a friend for a while. It's fun for life to be "apparently purposeless," for spontaneous connection and enjoyment to be purpose enough.

When we peer beneath the apparent mechanical humorlessness of the survival game, this is what we find: A world in which birds compete to produce rapturous melodies just for the fun of it. A world in which coyotes overturn hunters' traps because it's more fun than just avoiding them. A world in which even animals with highly rigid dominance hierarchies—fought for tooth and nail—find ways to set those hierarchies aside and goof around a while. A world in which the intimacy of contact is worth risking injury for, and is preceded by a reverent bow, a vulnerable invitation, that risky question: "Will you play with me?" A world in which even venomous snakes want only to seduce us into the unimaginable beauty of color vision, in which serendipitous mushrooms catapult us into imaginal encounters and catalyze our consciousness in the process. "The ultimate paradox," writes Burghardt, in the conclusion of his textbook on the science of play, "may be that play can only be understood through itself."[99]

4

On Formal Games,
or Containing the Mystery

For years I doubted and probed, until the decision had matured within me
and in spite of everything I decided in favor of the Game. I did so because I
had within me that urge to seek the supreme fulfillment and serve only the
greatest master.[1]

—MAGISTER LUDI, A CHARACTER IN
HERMANN HESSE'S *THE GLASS BEAD GAME*

I grant that you try to exalt this petty game into something akin to a sacrament, or at least to a device for edification. But sacraments do not spring from
such endeavors. The game remains a game.[2]

—FATHER JACOBUS, A CHARACTER IN
HERMANN HESSE'S *THE GLASS BEAD GAME*

THE ELEMENTS OF GAMES

So, what exactly is a game?

Unlike the ineffable, "I know it when I see it" quality of play, games
provide a framework around which play can be had, a formalization of
the boundaries set by the alpha wolf's playful bow, establishing that
what follows is removed from the stakes of life outside of the play.

Gallwey writes that "every game involves at least one player, a goal,
some obstacle between the player and his goal, a field (physical or

mental) on which the game is played and a motive for playing."[3] Working along similar lines, game researcher Jane McGonigal reduces every game to four basic elements: a goal, a set of rules, a feedback system, and voluntary participation.[4]

From here we can see that Huizinga's classic definition of play more closely resembles a definition of formal games. He seems to conflate the two when he writes that play is a "free activity standing quite consciously outside 'ordinary life' as being 'not serious,' but at the same time absorbing the player intensely and utterly . . . it proceeds within its own proper boundaries of time and space according to fixed rules and in an orderly manner."[5]

These "proper boundaries of time and space" establish a sense of order internal to the game. We know what the rules are, what the logic of the playground is. We know when and where the game will start and stop. This allows us to feel safe enough to let go and explore without having to worry about getting hurt in the process. When we trust our playmates, the desire to play may happily compel us to join in without having clearly defined the boundaries and navigated every possible scenario in advance. More explicit and agreed-upon rules broaden the pool of those with whom we are willing to play.

But whether we have explicitly reviewed each rule or dived right in, our participation in the game is contingent on our continued desire to play, which may be withdrawn at any time. At that time, it is no longer "play"—a sensation we learn as children at the moment roughhousing goes a step too far or when playful teasing strikes a nerve. If play is initiated as a ruse to hurt, you are unlikely to inhabit a playful world for long. The happening of a game is an ephemeral unfolding cocreated by the willing consent and participation of its players. By its own definition, it cannot be forced or obligated.

The English psychoanalyst Wilfred Bion referred to this sense of order as *containment* and argued it was essential to any genuinely transformative experience. A former tank commander in World War I, Bion may have been influenced by the physical containment of the tank itself, whose heavy metal walls insulated him from the chaotic violence of the surrounding war zone and so provided a sense of safety.

Translating this experience to the therapeutic process, Bion found that his clients would only feel safe enough to let their guard down in a physically and emotionally contained environment—one in which rules and boundaries were clear to everyone.

This same sense of containment is essential to unleashing our full potential in a game. The genius of a game is that, by combining a few simple elements within the structure of a container, it directs our engagement toward that involuntary rapture, that out-of-control feeling we all yearn for, while allowing us to enjoy the freefall, knowing we are safely strapped in for the ride. To step onto the field of a game, then, is to enter into a constructive relationship with the kind of power that, if uncontained, could destroy you, or radically transform you in the process.

GAMES AND THEIR TYPES

Eric Berne's theory of transactional analysis describes the unconscious games played between people in comparison to what types of games we are consciously aware of. We can then divide these into two categories.

The first type of game is overt and formal. It is overt in the sense that all players have openly acknowledged that they are playing a game and have freely agreed to play that game together. And it is formal in the sense that it has explicit objectives, known and shared by its players. Further, there may be explicit rules to how a player may achieve those objectives and clearly delineated boundaries, in which they agree to remain.

These characteristics describe a huge variety of games, from competitive sports like baseball or downhill skiing to tabletop competitions played with boards, cards, and dice and all the other activities that typically come to mind when we think of games. In fact, this first type of game is often the only activity we can think of when we think of games, for to acknowledge the existence of the second type is to violate its cardinal rule of secrecy and therefore risk cancellation from its arena of play.

This second type of game is covert and informal. It is covert in the sense that none of its players have acknowledged, even to themselves, that they are playing a game together. In many cases, if even one of the players were to acknowledge involvement in a game, the game would cease to continue—or at least cease to exist in its prior form. When we say that this game is informal, we mean it has implicit goals, rules, and boundaries, never spoken of directly, which the players must intuitively discern through trial and error and unconsciously remain within to continue their play. Examples include everything from relationship conflicts to chronic illnesses.

In dualistic aspects, we could even describe these as "masculine" and "feminine" forms of play and recognize that our general preconceptions of gender follow suit. Men, as a whole, are attracted to the overt competition and the trophies it offers. However, much of what we call "the real world," as opposed to the world of explicit games, falls within the boundaries of the more feminine form of play. And often, too, women express their mastery in navigating these subtle games with guile that outmatches their male counterparts. While these generalities may be most obvious in our awareness, neither gender is limited to or excluded from participating in these more or less explicit forms of the game.

In her discussion of the cultural bias against games, Jane McGonigal writes that "what we're really afraid of isn't games; we're afraid of losing track of where the game ends and where reality begins."[6] This fear underlies the artificial distinction between games and "the real world." For to acknowledge that life consists of a series of games is to acknowledge that we, at the very least, have the potential for freedom and creativity in areas where we have historically felt bounded, powerless, and at the mercy of an external constraint—that the grave seriousness of our dramas is merely an element of a theatrical performance, designed to lend potency and exhilaration to the covert games we play with ourselves and with others throughout our lives. "As players we conspire to give the game meaning," writes McGonigal, "to help each other get emotionally caught up in the act of playing."[7] And this is just as true in the playground of a divorce trial as on the battleground of the Wimbledon tennis championship.

THE INNER AND OUTER GAME

Let's start by looking at formal games, as they're more obvious to us, and their unambiguous rules make them easier to recognize and comprehend the mechanics of their components. Sports, bathed in spotlights and poured over by its voracious fans, make an ideal specimen to illuminate the elements of overt formal games.

In his classic book *The Inner Game of Tennis,* Timothy Gallwey draws a distinction between the inner and outer aspects of a game,[8] and their relationship as it is expressed through the structured play of overt games.

This distinction between inner and outer strikes at the heart of the transformational power of play. For the mystery of a game is that, by adding unnecessary external obstacles, it brings our unnecessary internal obstacles into focus—those impediments to the freest and truest, most organic expressions of our essential nature. The outer game provides the context in which we can come into relationship with these inner obstacles. We can face them, look them in the eye, and become intimate with how they express themselves in our thoughts, feelings, and actions. These emergent behaviors would only come to light in the heat and pressure of the game, and we can unify these warring elements of the psyche in the pursuit of our goal.

Consider Michael Jordan's experience in the 1991 NBA finals. Although he was widely viewed as one of the greatest players in the game, after six years in the NBA, Jordan still hadn't won a championship ring. To his coach Phil Jackson, the reason for this was obvious: Michael simply refused to include the rest of his teammates in his play.

This one-man-show playing style may have worked during the regular season, but it was failing every year during the playoffs—especially as teams designed defensive strategies to effectively shut him down. By the 1991 championships, it was clear to Michael that the outcome would either be a team victory for the Bulls or another personal failure.

Throughout the seven-game series, Jordan was often double-teamed by the opposing Lakers, though his skills still shone bright enough to power the Bulls to take the lead three games to one. But, by game five, the Lakers had begun to make a strong comeback and Jordan's solo strategy was losing its effectiveness.

"Who's open, M.J.?" coach Phil Jackson asked him in a tense time-out for the Bulls' side. Jordan had been double-teamed four games straight, necessarily leaving a Bulls player unguarded.

"Who's open?" Jackson asked again, looking straight into his player's eyes.

"Paxson," he replied.

"Okay, so find him."[9]

Back on the court, Jordan got the ball and, as usual, the Lakers' Magic Johnson left his man to double-team M.J. But this time, the blocks that had kept the ball locked in Jordan's hands came undone;

the desire for a championship overwhelmed the solitary, habitual game he had been playing up until that point. Paxson was wide open. Michael passed him the ball—and Paxson made the shot. Then he made another, and another, and another.

After four shots in a row, Jordan was warming up to the strategy. But when the Lakers drew the game to within two points, with just over a minute left, everyone still expected Michael to drive for the game-winning shot. "But instead, he was luring the defense in his direction and trying to create a shot for, yes, Paxson," Phil writes. "It was a sweet ending. John nailed the two-pointer and we went on to win, 108–101."[10]

BY FOCUSING ON THE INNER GAME—on overcoming his own internal obstacles of pride, need for control, and mistrust of others—Jordan was able to get out of his own way enough to finally win the outer game as well. In *Free Play: Improvisation in Life and Art*, the improvisational musician Stephen Nachmanovitch speaks to this dynamic when he writes that "each piece of music we play, each dance . . . each episode of life reflects our own mind back at us, complete with all its imperfections, exactly as it is."[11] Games provide a concentrated arena in which to explore these self-reflections, in connection with others and in a spirit of play.

If the reward of the inner game is self-knowledge and authentic self-expression, then we can reinterpret the setbacks, challenges, and frustrations of the game as the alchemical lead, the *prima materia* through which our unconscious reactions and buried feelings are seen for what they are and transmuted into creative insights and fuel for the game. "Once I recognized that deeply buried secrets in a competitor tend to surface under pressure," writes international chess master Josh Waitzkin, "my study of chess became a form of psychoanalysis. I unearthed my subtlest foibles through chess, and the link between my personal and artistic side was undeniable . . . invariably the chess moves paralleled the life moment. Whenever I noticed a weakness, I took it on."[12]

RULES

Attaining the goal of our game is challenging because of the constraints, or rules, that we freely agree to remain within as players. These rules often develop and evolve as the instances of the game are played. Soccer, for instance, began as an explicit, if informal, medieval game sometimes called "folk football," in which mobs from competing villages would attempt to get an inflated pig's bladder to their opponent's marker using any means possible. After being outlawed several times over the centuries, the Industrial Revolution gave rise to the advent of formal schooling, and those schools invited competitive sport as physical exercise. They set limitations to the barbarism of the game and formalized its specifics as different schools began to play against one another.[13]

Even in formal games where violence is allowed, there are still limitations on what kind of violence is permitted, and when. For example, in a boxing match, you may only punch your opponent during the timed rounds.

As with the goal, the specifics of these rules are ultimately arbitrary. All that matters is how effectively they can concentrate the energy, connectivity, and resourcefulness of the players. Games draw out our genius by putting us into conditions that are always just barely outside of our comfort zone, but still within the bounds of the possible. In fact, games extend the bounds of the possible, by putting us voluntarily into circumstances difficult enough to demand all our physical, mental, and emotional faculties.

To adhere to the rules of play, then, is to volunteer to be uncomfortable—to be placed under a strain, constricted and confined to a limited set of movements or channels through which we can express ourselves and engage.

The rules delineate the boundaries of what is inside and outside of the game. They underlie the conventional distinction between "games" and "the real world," which we have revised as the distinction between "this formal game" and the surrounding, covert games that we must, to the extent we can, eradicate from our awareness so that we can order our consciousness and freely play.

Sportswriter Sam Sheridan speaks to this when he says that "in sports, the real world is nominally held at bay, locked outside the stadium doors for the viewer. No one is starving in football, there is no genocide in baseball, no terrorism coverage on ESPN. We watch a game to escape from the news, from politics. The rules are clear, there's a winner and a loser, and everything is as fair as we can make it."[14]

At least, this is the case in theory. But, as Sheridan points out, these boundaries are still somewhat permeable to the outside world. "Barely beneath the surface," he writes, "sports are [also] about race and religion, class and poverty. Outside life squeezes in through the edges of the field and climbs in under the ropes."[15]

The 1974 prize fight between Muhammad Ali and George Foreman in Kinshasa, Zaire, illustrates this. Billed as the Rumble in the Jungle, this title fight was supercharged with racial and social tensions from the very beginning.

This was due to the backstory: Ali had been banned from the sport and stripped of his championship title in 1967 for refusing to comply with the draft, which would likely have sent him to fight in the Vietnam

War. When he finally got the green light to box again in 1970, he lost his comeback match against Joe Frazier, forcing him to compete against lower-ranking fighters for almost four years before getting another shot at the heavyweight title.

His conscientious objection to the Vietnam War and the draft had made Ali an international hero to the millions who had suffered under Western colonialism, military aggression, and racism around the world, So, when his shot at the title finally came, Ali wasn't going to squander it.

The cultural undertones of this historic fight were further elevated when the organizers hosted a three-day music festival, titled Zaire 74, leading up to the contest. The blues of B.B. King, the funk of James Brown, and the soul of Bill Withers shared a stage with native Congolese musicians in an extraordinary homecoming, setting the tone for the coming battle.

Although both boxers were black, the continent clearly saw Ali as its representative. "We knew Muhammad Ali as a boxer," says Malian actor Malick Bowens, "but more importantly for his political stance—when we saw that America was at war in a third world country, Vietnam, and that one of the children of the United States said, 'Me? You want me to go fight against the Viet Cong? Why should I fight against them? They haven't done anything against me.' For us, it was extraordinary to see that in the America of that time, someone could take such a position. He may have lost his title, he may have lost millions of dollars, but that's where he gained the esteem of millions of Africans."[16]

Foreman, on the other hand, was seen as an ambassador of the West. "He arrived with a dog, a German Shepherd, which immediately offended Africans, since the Belgians had used Shepherds as police dogs," says Malick.[17]

Though Foreman was heavily favored by nearly every boxing expert—including many in Ali's own training camp—Ali channeled the intensity of the cultural moment, converting its energy into raw power. "I'm gonna fight for the prestige, not for me, but to uplift my little brothers who are sleeping on concrete floors today in America," he said. "Black people who are living on welfare, black people who can't eat, black people who don't know no knowledge of themselves, black people who don't have no future. I want to win my title and walk down the alleys, sit on the garbage can with the wine-heads. I want to walk down the street with the dope addicts, talk to the prostitutes, so I can help a lot of people . . . All I've got to do is whup George Foreman."[18]

The ensuing battle was a fight for the ages. Ali came out swinging in the first round, catching Foreman with a series of right-hand lead punches. But the punches didn't knock Foreman out; instead, they merely infuriated him. Ali spent the next few rounds with his back against the ropes, slipping in and out of Foreman's punches, tiring him out. "From the fifth round on, Ali went back on the offensive, lighting Foreman up with dizzying combinations amidst their mutual exhaustion. One such combination near the end of the eighth round sent Foreman whirling toward the ground—knocking him out, and restoring the world heavyweight championship belt to Muhammad Ali, the greatest there ever was."

So much for watching a game to escape from politics.

Yet even in a match as socially charged as the Rumble in the Jungle, all that energy still had to be filtered and expressed through the rules of the game, which dictated how it could be used. No amount of racial tension could have allowed Ali to take a swing at Foreman below the belt, or allowed Foreman to continue the fight on the street the next day. The rules were still the rules, clearly agreed upon in advance, and played within faithfully.

This is what James Carse means when he says that "a game occurs within a world." The players have agreed upon a shared set of values and have collectively constructed a bounded reality in which those values can be pursued. The temporal and spatial boundaries of the playtime and the playing field create a world with its own rules, roles, and aims. The developmental psychologist Michael Tomasello refers to this uniquely human ability to come together and strive toward an agreed-upon goal, within the boundaries of a world and its rules, as shared intentionality. "When we have shared intentionality," writes McGonigal, "we actively identify as part of a group, we deliberately and explicitly agree on a goal, and we can understand what others expect us to do in order to work toward that goal."[19] Shared intentionality informs our capacity to come together and conspire to bring a value-laden world into being, to speak an unformed possibility into a collective experience. The deeper this world-creating union is achieved, the more creative potential can be accessed and unleashed by the players, both teammates and competitors.

Within the confines of this world, actions are filtered through the agreed-upon values and, so, take on a meaning that would otherwise be inaccessible, providing each player with a fresh context in which to explore who they are, separate from the received values of the larger culture and its implicit game structure.

Even competition is a form of collaboration in that it rests upon certain shared agreements: The players agree to play within the rules, and, if only implicitly, to play their very best; to challenge the other as much as they can; to make the game so difficult for the opponent that they are drawn into otherwise unreachable depths.

GOAL

Simply put, the goal is the target of the players' actions, "the specific outcome the players will work to achieve."[20] Ultimately, the content of this goal itself is arbitrary—it might be to get this ball into that net or to configure these pieces such that the opponent's king can't escape. All that matters is that the players come together freely, determine that their goal is meaningful, and agree to invest their energy toward the fulfillment of that goal—typically while inhibiting their opponent's ability to do so.

The goal "continually orients their participation throughout the game," writes McGonigal. It "provides the players with a sense of purpose."[21] Players come together and pour themselves wholeheartedly into the fulfillment of the game's goal, often stretching themselves far beyond what they could otherwise imagine. The simple clarity of the goal, and the players' commitment to strive toward it, is what "unites them in pursuit of the impossible."

When it comes to utilizing the game as a laboratory for consciousness, the clarity of our goal is key. For "clarity gives us certainty," writes Steven Kotler. "We know what to do and we know where to focus our attention while doing it."[22] Kotler's years of studying flow states have yielded the insight that "when the brain is charged with a clear goal, focus narrows considerably, the unimportant is disregarded, and the now is all that's left."[23]

Each time we concentrate all our energy toward a clear goal in this way, we experience a restructuring and reordering of consciousness that persists long after the episode is over. "When we choose a goal and invest ourselves in it to the limits of our concentration," writes Csikszentmihalyi, "whatever we do will be enjoyable. And once we have tasted this joy, we will redouble our efforts to taste it again. This is the way the self grows."[24]

Clear goals marshal all our attention, drawing the mind and body into a unified and concentrated whole: The electric pulsing of our skin informs the thoughts that enter our awareness, and the richness of our feelings overlaps seamlessly with the singularity of our intentions. Through the simple act of orienting ourselves toward a clear and voluntary goal that is both challenging enough to engage us but not so challenging as to be genuinely insurmountable, everything falls into place: Action unifies with awareness, time dilates, the inner tyrant of the mind slips away, and we find ourselves possessed by that autotelic rapture characteristic of the deepest play.

TOMASELLO'S SCIENCE OF shared intentionality has huge ramifications for the business world as well. More than ever, companies need teams that can respond flexibly to their competitors and collaborate effectively to generate innovation. Just as in a game, the best way to activate this kind of performance is by combining clear goals with a sense of psychological safety. That means everyone on the team needs to know what they're aiming at, and, just as important, they need to feel safe enough to risk untried ways of getting there—exploring untapped possibilities, exposing hidden options, and recombining elements in novel acts of bricolage. "You want people who can challenge each other," says Ann Cairns, executive vice chair at MasterCard, but "they've got to feel safe."[25]

In most large companies, bureaucracy prevents these collaborative conditions from ever forming. Endless meetings, linear timelines, and short-term performance metrics interfere with the messy, squiggly business of innovation, whose logic can only be explained after the fact. In 1980, Semco, a Brazilian corporation whose factories produce everything from digital scanners to commercial dishwashers, took a radical approach to addressing this bureaucracy.

"When Ricardo Semler took over the company from his father," writes psychologist Keith Sawyer, "Semco was on the verge of bankruptcy, barely holding on with short-term bank loans, and Semler knew he had to do something radical. He began by firing most of the old-style senior managers on his first day."[26]

By gutting the entire company of its bureaucratic structure, Semler freed up its employees to reorganize themselves in a more fluid, dynamic fashion, with teams that "form and reform, their structure emerging improvisationally from the bottom up, and membership [that's] largely self-selected," writes Sawyer. "Although no boss is looking over your shoulders, the peer pressure to perform is intense: if you don't have the respect of your coworkers, you won't be selected to serve on any of the teams, and you're on your way out of the company."[27]

The plan worked. Sawyer reports that, "soon after Semco took on its new fluid organizational structure, it began to grow—faster than almost every other Brazilian company. By 2003, Semco's annual revenue had risen from $4 million to $212 million."[28]

FEEDBACK SYSTEM

A game's feedback system lets us know how effectively our play is moving us toward our goal. This could be as simple as the point system in a basketball game or the ringing in your ears after a hard jab in a boxing match. What matters most, writes Csikszentmihalyi, is "the symbolic message it contains: that I have succeeded in my goal. Such knowledge creates order in consciousness and strengthens the structure of the self."[29]

Feedback keeps up the pace and intensity of a game by giving the players moment-by-moment information on the quality of their play, driving them deeper into engagement with their activity in the process.

Absent this kind of feedback, the mind has a tendency to leave the immediacy of the moment and wander into the past or future in search of information to evaluate itself against. "If we can't course correct in real time," writes Kotler, "we start looking for clues to better performance—things we did in the past, things we've seen other people do, things that can pull us out of the moment. When feedback is immediate, the information required is always close at hand."

Research conducted by neuroscientist Judy Willis on the role of feedback in games reveals the mechanism underlying this process. "When you have constant opportunities to try different strategies and get feedback," she writes, "you get more frequent and intense bursts of dopamine," which improves attention, helps integrate information, and happens to feel wonderful. "Not only do you get minute-to-minute pleasure, but the mindset starts changing in long-term ways. Your brain starts looking at things that weren't achievable before and starts to think they might be achievable with a little effort. It expects to learn and improve and eventually succeed."[30] The more real-time this feedback system is, the more dopamine is released into the brain. "Scientists know that dopamine is released every time we anticipate feedback from a goal-oriented action," writes McGonigal, "we get a rush of excitement to find out how we did."[31]

VOLUNTARY PARTICIPATION

Here again we encounter the dictum that "whoever plays, plays freely, and whoever must play cannot play." Voluntary participation is the only difference between the terror of a kidnapping and the exhilaration of an escape room or in the context of a BDSM role-play scenario. In both the escape room and BDSM play, consent is a fundamental principle to ensure the safety of the participants. The rules and the boundaries—the delineated world of the game—make it easier for us to say yes to its uncertainty, knowing that this uncertainty is bounded. We can choose to enter into uncomfortable conditions, knowing that the risks are explicit and can be evaluated, or negotiated, beforehand. The boundedness of a game in time, space, and number allows us to decide in advance whether we are willing to play *this* game at *this* time in *this* place with *this* number of people. Along the way, we get to practice relating to the game's challenges as creative opportunities. As we internalize this process of reframing obstacles as triggers for expanded awareness, we can begin to allow our container to widen—for our play to occur in a longer time, a vaster space, with more players, and under more conditions. For the boundaryless player of the game of life, the universe of Lila is itself one big container—containing us in the loving arms of the divine—and every challenge, however uncomfortable, is remembered and experienced as a part of the play, voluntarily chosen by the divinity in us that wants to know what it feels like to become intimate with the full spectrum of experience.

Consider the life of Garchen Rinpoche, a Tibetan monk and mystic. After being taken to the Lho Miyalgon monastery at the age of seven, the young Rinpoche began a life of rigorous meditation training. But his training was cut short when, at the age of twenty-two, the Chinese communist army invaded Tibet and sent him away to a prison labor camp.

After several years of imprisonment, Rinpoche developed a serious illness and was sent to the prison hospital. Rather than eating the food they served him, however, he chose to give his portion away to the other inmates—a crime for which he was sent to solitary confinement.

For whatever reason, the head of the hospital decided one day to come visit him in his solitary cell. "At that time, I was lying in the bed, and very weak, and could not move. So I asked him to come closer," recalls Rinpoche. The hospital head "came closer and closer, and when he was really close, I spat on his face and punched him."[32]

To Rinpoche's surprise, rather than ordering him to be killed on the spot, the official burst into laughter. He then wrote a letter to the cooks saying that they should give Rinpoche whatever food he wanted, in whatever quantity, until he recovered. "Day by day I got better. After one month I recovered and was able to get back up again," says Rinpoche. "I wondered why he had that much compassion for me."[33]

The prison guards then returned him to the labor camp, where he met the man who would become his spiritual master: Khenpo Munsel Rinpoche. "I heard you punched that official," Khenpo Munsel said, in their first meeting. "You have learned how to take suffering as the path. . . . Out of concern for others, you gave up even the thought of your own life, and that if they kill you that is alright. There was no self-grasping, no thought of, 'What will happen to me?'"[34]

Khenpo Munsel then offered Garchen Rinpoche the first of many spiritual instructions: "In that moment of anger, instead of looking at that person or what made you angry, look at the anger itself. . . . When the anger arises, realize that self and other do not exist and are not separate. This dualistic perception of self and other is a delusion."[35]

"Before I got those teachings," says Rinpoche, "I saw practice and the [prison] work I had to do as separate. I was angry with that official and punched him, and he had great compassion and love for me, and that was what caused my mind to feel more relaxed. That is why we say, in the bodhisattva path, we transform the affliction through love and compassion . . . that is what I learned from Khenpo Munsel Rinpoche."[36]

Garchen Rinpoche continued to practice sincerely in this way for the duration of his imprisonment, taking every injustice, every cause for anger and outrage, every dehumanizing incident as fuel for the cultivation of his consciousness. He did not let the communist army deprive him of his monastic training. On the contrary, he used the horrific conditions of his imprisonment as a container in which to deepen his practice by exposing him to feelings and triggers that could not have been provided by even the finest preinvasion monasteries.

Khenpo Rinpoche's advice steered Garchen Rinpoche's mind toward the obstacle, anger, challenging him to master it. In his pursuit to realize the nondualism between himself and the Chinese guards, he also dissolved the separation between prison work and his Buddhist practice. Viewed through the lens of a game, we could say that Garchen Rinpoche expanded the boundaries of his game to incorporate the guards as players and the prison yard as an expanded field of play. This is not to dismiss the seriousness of his situation—the stakes were as high as they had ever been—but by voluntarily engaging with his circumstance as a game, Garchen Rinpoche found freedom and the opportunity for mastery within his restricted surroundings.

Naturally, not every one of us is an incarnate Tibetan master, prepared to take the container of a prison camp as a tantric Buddhist playground. It may take the boundaries of an explicit, formal game to match the particular level of pressure and containment that would allow us to soften the rigidity of our identity—with its need for comfort, predictability, and security—without pushing us so hard that we go into survival mode. We can enjoy the roller coaster of a single game, knowing we are safely strapped in for the ride. But at each ride's peak, we may catch a glimpse of the possibility beyond, the playing field inhabited by our entire incarnation, held just as tightly by the arms of the divine.

LIBERATING THE INNER SELF

Game provides a path through which to liberate the true self from the grip of the false ego. For the master players seek not merely to win the outer game, but to pierce the furthest recesses of their heart and soul in the process—to surrender themselves to the demands of their art, to recover themselves from the demands of their persona.

When we throw ourselves into the arena of play with full abandon, we find that our movements become orchestrated by a creative intelligence, an emergent wisdom—by the spirit of play itself. The paradox is that, by turning ourselves over to this intelligence, we are drawn deeper into union with the truth of who we are. We set our inner genius free and allow it to swing our limbs with the elegance of a master conductor, conducting the electricity that wants nothing more than to flow through us. "No longer conscious of my movement," writes Bannister, after breaking the four-minute mile, "I discovered a new unity with nature. I had found a new source of power and beauty, a source I never dreamt existed."[37]

To be a master player is to live from a state of surrendered devotion to this life force and the unimaginable power and beauty that it affords. Through our continual immersion into the heat of the game, we melt off the impediments to the free flow of this power and allow it to restore us to our original nature. As the distance between spirit and skin begins to vanish, and the interval between player and game begins to disappear, we find ourselves winning the outer game, too, and with an otherwise inaccessible ease and clarity. "Perhaps the most decisive element of my game," writes Waitzkin, "was that my style on the board was completely in sync with my personality. . . . I was unhindered by internal conflict—a state of being that I have come to see as essential."[38]

The alternative is to fixate entirely on the outer game—on aiming at the target, while forgetting to aim at ourselves. When we do so, we often find that our play draws us further away from the truth of who we are. We leave the authentic self behind and grasp the false security of theories and strategies in hopes that they will carry us across the perilous waters of the deep game. As the turbulence increases in its intensity, we drift progressively further from our essential nature, from the genius that could and would provide a creative solution to the challenges of the moment—if only it were invoked.

Waitzkin frames this as the difference between a universal and a stylized player. Using jiujitsu world champion Marcelo Garcia to illustrate the distinction, he tells us that Marcelo "doesn't study his opponent and shut him down. Instead, he expresses his game. He makes you play with him. A universal player observes the opponent's rhythms and builds a game plan around it," whereas a stylized player draws the opponent into the center of his being.[39]

The distinction comes through clearly in Marcelo's approach to preparing for competition. Waitzkin tells us that, unlike most competitors, who kept their training programs a secret, Marcelo streamed his sparring sessions every night during the lead-up to big tournaments. Rather than keeping his techniques to himself, Marcelo openly displayed the moves he planned to use against his opponents for weeks in advance. As far as he was concerned, anyone who studied his game would be entering his domain, and he'd always be better at his own game than anyone else.[40]

The chess Grandmaster Tigran Petrosian devised a similarly brilliant approach to stylized play. Waitzkin writes that when Petrosian was competing in major tournaments, he would start each morning by "sitting quietly in his room for a period of introspection. His goal was to observe his mood down to the finest nuance."[41] Only after taking this time to become as attuned to his inner world as possible would he begin to design his game plan. "If he was feeling cautious, quiet, not overwhelmingly confident, he tended to choose an opening that took fewer risks and led to a position that harmonized with his disposition. If feeling energized, aggressive, exceedingly confident, he would pick an opening that allowed him to express himself in a more creative vein . . . instead of imposing an artificial structure on his match strategy, Petrosian tried to be as true to himself as possible on a moment-to-moment basis. He believed that if his mood and the chess position were in sync, he would be most inclined to play with the greatest inspiration."[42]

EMERGENT GENIUS

There is a delicate balance involved in this art: For our aim is to lose our conditioned self in the constraints of the game, such that our unconditioned self can rise up to take its place. Too much self, and the game cannot saturate us enough to work its magic; too much game, and our true nature cannot enter into the play.

But when multiple players come together and strike this tenuous balance, something extraordinary can occur. For the synergy between the players and the game can immerse them into much deeper states of flow than would otherwise be accessible. Psychologists refer to this as group flow: A state in which each player's genius emerges to meet the genius in the other, collaboratively and improvisationally. "It's a peak state," writes psychologist Keith Sawyer in his book *Group Genius*. "In situations of rapid change, it's more important than ever for a group to be able to merge action and awareness, to adjust immediately by improvising."[43]

Group flow allows us to set aside our cognitive filters—which are far too slow to rely on without the thread of the game slipping out from between our fingers—and participate in a bottom-up, self-organizing system: an emergent mystery, an expression of the sacred.

Scientists have, in recent years, begun to map out the biology beneath these mystical states of play. In a series of experiments conducted by Dr. Michiel Savijarvi-Spapé and Dr. Niklas Rajava, the investigators concluded that when two people are playing a game together, they enter a state of "neurological and psychological linkage."[44] Summarizing these findings, McGonigal writes that "the two players start to make the same facial expressions, smiling and frowning in unison. Their heart rates adapt to the same rhythm. Their breathing patterns sync. Most astonishingly, their brain waves sync, as their neurons start to 'mirror' each other—a process that helps each of them anticipate what the other will do next. All these changes happen almost immediately, within minutes of starting to play."[45]

Savijarvi-Spapé and Rajava discovered that these linkages take place regardless of whether the players are on the same or opposing team. "Any game played simultaneously by two people in the same physical location creates this . . . kind of 'mind melt' and body synchronization," writes McGonigal, through which "we're able to anticipate each other's actions."[46]

Navy SEALs have discovered that they can deepen this physical and mental synchronization by continually surrendering to the shifting needs of the moment. In *Stealing Fire,* Kotler and Wheal quote the Navy SEAL Rich Davis, who says that "when SEALs sweep a building . . . the person who knows what to do next is the leader. We're entirely nonhierarchical in that way. . . . In a combat environment, when split seconds make all the difference, there's no time for second-guessing. When someone steps up to become the new leader, everyone, immediately, automatically, moves with him. It's the only way we win."[47] Whether in the life-or-death context of a war game or the heightened rapture of an Olympic final, the principle therefore remains the same: When we surrender to the spirit of the game and allow it to direct our steps, it will guide us into union with ourselves, with others, and with the transcendent beauty of our symphonic play.

By dissolving our separateness in this way, group flow allows us to intuit what Martin Luther King Jr. spoke of spiritually when he said that "in a real sense, all of life is interrelated . . . All persons are caught in an inescapable network of mutuality, tied in a single garment of destiny. Whatever affects one directly affects all indirectly. I can never be what I ought to be until you are what you ought to be, and you can never be what you ought to be until I am what I ought to be. This is the interrelated structure of reality."[48]

To be a master player in the truest sense of the word, then, is to enter into a service position: We pursue the fullest expression of ourselves by encouraging the fullest expression of others. We find the point at which integration begets differentiation, and separation induces union. We hang on to our allotted thread in the interwoven garment of destiny and allow it to weave us straight into the center of our divinity. In *The Glass Bead Game*, Hermann Hesse writes that "the dark interior, the esoterics of the Game, points down into the One and All, into those depths where the eternal Atman eternally breathes in and out, sufficient unto itself. One who had experienced the ultimate meaning of the Game within himself would . . . [therefore] no longer dwell in the world of multiplicity . . . since he would know altogether different joys and raptures."[49]

STRETCHING FIBERS, PULLING THREADS

This descent into the One and All, into the esoterics of the Game, requires a willingness to inhabit increasingly uncomfortable conditions and learn to cultivate facility there. Consider the case of Nino Shembri, a jiujitsu player: when Sheridan asked him how he got so good at sub-mitting his opponents from unconventional or awkward positions, Nino replied that he simply inventoried all of the places in which he was weakest, all the positions he would reflexively avoid, and then put all of his energy into finding freedom in those locations. "He doesn't fight to get into the right positions," writes Sheridan. "He learns and practices submissions from positions he's uncomfortable in."[50]

When we stretch ourselves to our limits in this way, we find that what appeared to be a solid barrier transforms, through the intimacy of contact, into a flexible boundary—more permeable and negotiable than we could have imagined. But this flexibility will only open itself to us when we risk pushing past the limits of impossibility, when we dissolve the boundaries of our self-definition such that something deeper can reveal itself. For "if you aren't in over your head," writes T.S. Eliot, "how do you know how tall you are?"[51]

Tennis champions Rafael Nadal and Novak Djokovic experienced this firsthand during the 2012 Australian Open. When the rivals faced off in the finals match, everyone expected a grueling battle. But no one could have anticipated that the game would drag on for nearly six hours—longer than any other match in tennis history. "You're going through so much suffering your toes are bleeding," says Djokovic. "Everything is just outrageous, but you're still enjoying that pain."[52]

As they moved through these layers of suffering and fatigue, the players were forced to draw from deeper reservoirs of power to over-come their opponent: Djokovic, for example, went from kissing the crucifix around his neck to praying aloud in the middle of the court. "I was trying to find every possible help and energy that I possibly can," he says. "It paid off, I guess."[53] Because at 1:37 in the morning, he pre-vailed over Nadal.

The psychologist William James lends scientific insight into this kind of endurance when he writes that "fatigue gets worse up to a certain critical point, when gradually or suddenly it passes away, and we are fresher than before. We have evidently tapped a level of new energy, masked until then by the fatigue-obstacle usually obeyed. There may be layer after layer of this experience."[54] His language is illuminating: For, when we are under the sway of our limited preconceptions, then the obstacle becomes the master, the object of our obedience. We subordinate ourselves to the finite density of our circumstances, forgetting that those circumstances are intermixed with our projections of who we think we are and what we think we're capable of. In doing so, we block the rise of our own genius, the part of us that could and would make light of those obstacles—moving under, over, or even straight through them in the course of its play.

But when we orient ourselves toward this inner master and follow it into the unknown, then "we may find," continues James, "beyond the very extremity of fatigue-distress, amounts of power and ease that we never dreamed ourselves to own, sources of strength habitually not taxed at all, because habitually we never push through the obstruction, never pass those early critical points."[55] Building on this insight, the motocross rider Travis Pastrana says that "every good athlete can find flow, but it's what you do with it that makes you great. If you consistently use that state to do the impossible, you get confident in your ability to do the impossible. You begin to expect it."[56]

There is, however, an art to this limit-stretching. The idea is not simply to blow past our range, but to live in the possibility that many of our perceived limitations may be self-imposed constructs. We aim for that sweet spot, where the body and mind will stretch but not snap. We find the line, and then we decide, in the words of BASE jumper Miles Daisher, to "tickle it a bit. And then [we] find out that's not actually the line. The impossible is actually a little farther out, so let's go over there and tickle it again."[57]

We stretch the horizon of the possible by engaging with challenges just barely outside of our comfort zone. As for how far exactly: "answers vary," writes Kotler, "but the general thinking is about 4 percent. That's it. That's the sweet spot. If you want to trigger flow, the challenge should be 4 percent greater than the skills."[58] The idea is to stretch ourselves far enough to trigger dopamine, which "heightens attention and pattern recognition," but not so far that we are taken out of the present moment and into our fears about the cost of failure.[59] "the road to real magic," writes Kotler, involves pushing 4 percent further than we did the day before, "day after day, week after week. . . . Follow this path long enough, and not only does impossible become possible, it becomes what's next."[60]

Waitzkin refers to this process as "an exploration of grayness" and highlights the artful balance between pushing yourself relentlessly, but not so hard that you melt down.[61] The key word here is "exploration," for an exploration of grayness is an exploration in the sense that it involves genuine uncertainty. We really don't know what our limits are. We don't know what positions we can and cannot cultivate freedom in. We don't even know the limits on the types of questions we can ask in pursuit of this exploration. To explore the grayness, then, is to explore every weird permutation of movement, to invert every convention, deconstruct every orthodoxy, doubt every impossibility, and do so with the freedom and levity characteristic of the play spirit. For it is a matter of taste whether or not a movement is genuinely harmful or an obstacle is genuinely insurmountable. "If we feel free enough," writes Nachmanovitch, "we may even play in the face of great danger."[62]

THE ENEMY IS THE FRIEND

In this way, our opponents become our greatest friends. The rules and goals of the game channel us toward each other, revealing an intimacy born of competition. They challenge our perceived physical and psychological limits, revealing to us our full creative potential. For our skill can only rise in proportion to the difficulty of the obstacle presented to us, and no one is more committed to posing those challenges than our opponent. "Only by playing the role of the enemy does he become your true friend," writes Gallwey. "It is the duty of the opponent to create the greatest possible difficulties for you, just as it is yours to try to create obstacles for him. Only by doing this do you give each other the opportunity to find out to what heights each can rise."[63]

Within the bounded world of a formal game, our enemies stand ready to crash upon us at the first wrong move, at the first lapse of our concentration. They continually demand our sharpest precision, subtlest perception, nimblest movement of body and mind. They flood into our game and wash away the sediments of conditioned responses and received limitations, driving us into the hidden pathways through which we can overcome their power. Waitzkin speaks to this when he writes: "From one perspective, the opponent is the enemy. On the other there is no one who knows you more intimately, no one who challenges you so profoundly or pushes you to excellence and growth so relentlessly. Sitting at the chessboard, just feet away from the other, you can hear every breath, feel every quiver, sense any flicker of fear or exhilaration. Hours pass with your entire being tapped into your opponent's psyche, while the other follows your thoughts like a shadow and yearns for your demise."[64]

We come to know ourselves most intimately through our reflection in our enemies. For they mirror back to us our every contradiction, our every impediment to free movement and unobstructed play. Without the challenges they ruthlessly impose upon us, we would be terribly limited in our capacity to know and express ourselves fully as players. This awareness allows us to recognize the meaning of every game master's hidden prayer: May the enemy grow stronger, faster, more resourceful and creative, more insidious, relentless, merciless, and punishing. May the enemy continue to drive me into every corner of my being, so that I may discover the hidden solubility of my perceived limitations. "Instead of hoping your opponent is going to double-fault," writes Gallwey, this prayer has us "actually wish that he'll get his first serve in. This desire for the ball to land inside the line helps you to achieve a better mental state for returning it."[65]

The basketball player Bill Russell makes a similar confession, saying that he "sometimes secretly rooted for the opposing team during big games, because if they were doing well, it meant he would have a more heightened experience."[66]

To be a true friend, we have a responsibility to play to our opponents' weaknesses, to torture them as an act of devotion to the genius in them that would rise only under a certain intensity of heat and pressure—like those towering redwoods that can only germinate after a forest fire.

In other words, we do our opponents a disservice by hesitating to expose their weaknesses. To refrain from touching the most vulnerable places in their psyche and not to engage the least sturdy aspects of their game are akin to withholding love. Out of devotion to the latent genius in them that wants nothing more than to express itself, we become willing to assume the role of enemy and even take on the other player's villainizing projections—should the overcoming of those projections, of the demon we have become for them, draw out more of their creative energy and primal power.

The Dalai Lama refers to this as "the enemy's gift," for it is only by being continuously wounded by the one that would live as our shadow that we can come into true intimacy with ourselves and our power.[67]

The enemy's gift is that they are willing to be merciless with us, and that they will not even consider the notion that we could be victimized by their play. "In order to practice sincerely and to develop patience," writes the Dalai Lama, "you need someone who willfully hurts you. Thus, these people give us real opportunities to practice these things. They are testing our inner strength in a way that even our guru cannot."[68]

Although the magic circle of the game, its rules, and its goals, provides the containment for our play, it is the enemy that brings the necessary ingredient for that play to be alchemical—for it to purify us of even the subtlest impediments to freedom. The enemy is the one who holds us to the fire and laughs as we melt into the essence of our divinity. They draw us into the hot, molten core of our being and know precisely the heat, pressure, and intensity required to take us there.

ON UNCONTAINED CHAOS, OR ALCHEMIZING BOUNDARY TRANSGRESSIONS

As our concept of the enemy as a friend expands, so too does our capacity to receive the enemy's gifts, irrespective of the form or context in which they are presented. This brings us to the distinction between an enemy and a boundary transgressor: Whereas enemies, for all their ruthlessness, will always uphold the shared agreements of the game, boundary transgressors will respect nothing but their desire to win at any cost. Rather than playing to our vulnerabilities within the rule structure of the game, they play with the inherent vulnerabilities of that structure itself. By playing *with* the rules rather than *within* the rules, boundary transgressors challenge us to further stretch the limitations on our play.

Boundary transgressors are threatening because they introduce more chaos into the game than the other players had initially agreed to. They bring more unpredictability, more access to the unknown, and so more risk. Like the cross-dressing coyote of our Nez Perce tale (in chapter 3), this kind of player has no regard whatsoever for either the welfare of the opponent or the ethical system within which that opponent is confined. For this reason, most conventional players tend to demonize boundary transgressors and treat them as enemies of the game. But their demonization and slander tend not to impede boundary transgressors play at all, for these verbal attacks derive their power from the same rule structure that they themselves don't take seriously.

THERE ARE FOUR MAIN WAYS of responding to such a transgressive playing style. The first is to experience yourself as a victim and petition for an outside authority—like a referee or a commissioner—to rescue you. This is the most typical response. When players assume the victim role, they will often put on a show of helplessness in order to enroll others into expelling the transgressor from the arena of play. This victim response demonstrates that the player does not know how to engage with someone who plays with the rules, for as Carse writes, "It is by knowing what the rules are that we know what the game is."[69] Finding themselves thrown into a game about which they know little and within which they feel inexperienced, confused, and threatened, these players will do everything they can to pause the game until the anomaly is removed and the play can return to "its proper boundaries of space and time according to fixed rules and in an orderly manner."

The second response is to violate the transgressor's own boundaries in return. For example, if the transgressor continually elbows a player on the basketball court, that player might begin to elbow him back as well. Or if the transgressor hits an opponent in sensitive areas such as the groin or breasts during a wrestling match, the opponent may hit back in kind. Although superficially this may appear to be more potent than the first response, it is still fundamentally rooted in victimhood: Rather than attacking the transgressor by petitioning outside authorities, the player simply attacks the transgressor in the same way the player felt attacked. The player's values are thus abandoned in order to meet the transgressor with the same violence. In doing so, the player forfeits the promise of the inner game that could have drawn both parties into union with the authenticity of their being. By resorting to these methods, they lose touch with themselves inwardly and at the outer game as well—for the transgressor will always be more experienced at violation than the player.

The third response is to carry on with your play as if the transgressions were not occurring. This is the denial response, and it similarly alienates the player from the authenticity of the experience. Acting as a buffer between external presentation and internal feelings, this response inevitably results in a numbing of the player's senses. When a player acts from a place of denial, the player's movements become awkward, dissociated, distracted, and disengaged. Creative energy is sapped out of the arena of play and poured into the emotional and mental walls the player must maintain as insulation from the fear, rage, helplessness, and other feelings elicited by the transgression.

The boundaryless nature of the transgressor's play often escalates the provocations. If the initial transgressions do not elicit the desired response, the transgressor will simply increase the intensity of these transgressions until succeeding in destabilizing the opponent and winning the game.

The fourth response is to channel the intense feelings elicited by the transgressor into our play and use them as creative fuel. This is the mastery response. When a player has the freedom to alchemize violation in this way, he can unleash unprecedented reservoirs of power into the game. The Olympic wrestling champion Dan Gable illustrates this mastery when he says that "if I knew the guy was on steroids, that would *help* me. . . . Whereas some might think, 'Oh, he's cheating,' or 'He's got an unfair advantage,' for me you didn't pay the price. You're not as committed as I am. . . . He may be strong, but all I have to do . . . is loosen one single wire in his brain, make him do something that isn't perfect, and he'll fall apart."[70]

In this brilliant inversion, Gable turns the advantage afforded by the transgressor against him by treating it as evidence of spiritual weakness and mental laziness. The key lies in Gable's ability to utilize the energetic charge of the transgression without being mentally hooked by the thought that it "shouldn't be happening" or "is unfair." He takes the transgression and turns it against the transgressor, galvanizing his own play in the process.

In *The Art of Learning,* Waitzkin illustrates the process of moving through these stages—from victimhood to denial to integrated power—first during his time as a professional chess player, and later during his career as a competitive martial artist. Waitzkin writes that when he represented the United States in international chess tournaments, his Russian opponents would often cheat. These kids "were great players who presented a whole new set of challenges, [but] instead of adapting and raising their games, American kids dropped out."[71]

One of these transgressors would often get up from the chessboard mid-game to discuss "the position in Russian with his coach, a famous grandmaster. There were complaints, but little was done to stop the cheating. No one could prove what was discussed because of the language barrier, and the truth is that it didn't even matter. While valuable chess ideas might have been exchanged, the psychological effect was much more critical."[72]

In this case, the American kids played the victim by acting helpless and petitioning to the authorities to rescue them from the Russian transgressors. When these petitions failed to remove the transgressors from the game, the players withdrew themselves from the game instead: For they could not imagine playing the game in this new, expanded form, with the transgressors' added complexity and risk. To preserve the game they loved, these players believed they needed to leave it.

Rather than taking this victim approach, Waitzkin initially opted for denial: He attempted to suppress his feelings and proceed as though the transgressions weren't occurring. "The problem with this approach is that [his rival] Boris didn't have a limit. He was perfectly content to escalate the situation . . . and eventually I would get pissed off and have a meltdown."[73] These experiences alerted Waitzkin to the need to learn to harness and channel the rage that Boris's transgressions were triggering in him. But it wasn't until years later, during his career as a martial artist, that he found a way to deliberately practice this skill—to foster the movement from denial to mastery, from resisting an uncomfortable feeling to surrendering to the latent power that it harbored.

The opportunity came when he was competing in his first Tai Chi Chuan Push Hands National Championship. During one of the key matches, his opponent repeatedly violated the rules by headbutting Waitzkin in the nose. This blatant transgression triggered him so deeply that he nearly lost the match. It inspired him to learn to grapple with these dirty moves in a deeper way—as he would surely encounter more of them in the future. So, he began to seek "out dirty players and got better and better at keeping cool when they got out of control."[74]

One of these players, a martial artist from his school he called Frank, used to strike at his neck whenever their sparring matches would start to turn in Waitzkin's favor. Up until this point, Waitzkin had mostly avoided training with Frank. But, after his experience at the Nationals, he decided that Frank would be the perfect partner to practice the art of transforming violation into power. "I quickly realized that the reason I got angry when he went after my neck was that I was scared," he writes. "I didn't know how to handle it and thought I would get hurt. He was playing outside of the rules so a natural defense mechanism of mine was anger and righteous indignation, just like with Boris."[75]

But, unlike with Boris, Waitzkin was able to design a training program entirely around the kind of violations that Frank was so masterful at. He started by asking a trustworthy partner to target his neck during their sparring matches, so he could get used to defending against them without feeling like he was in real danger. Then, whenever Frank would show up, he would seek him out as a training partner and see if he could defend against his neck attacks.

It turned out that, without the emotional fluster of the situation, Waitzkin had no problem defending against Frank's neck attacks. Though Frank would escalate the situation by attacking other vulnerable areas like the groin, Waitzkin still managed to stick to his intention to stay "cool under increasingly bad conditions."[76] Having recontextualized these violations as part of the game, he was no longer thrown when they occurred.

Once he got used to staying cool under pressure, Waitzkin deepened his game by allowing himself to heat up under pressure—but to do so consciously. Rather than being blinded by rage, he allowed his feelings to flood into his body, electrify his cells, and inform his every movement. Waitzkin writes that this was "more about sweeping away the cobwebs than about learning anything new. We are built to be sharpest when in danger, but protected lives have distanced us from our natural abilities to channel our energies. Instead of running from our emotions or being swept away by their initial gusts," he encourages us to "learn to sit with them, become at peace with their unique flavors, and ultimately discover deep pools of inspiration."[77]

This is the path to play mastery: We draw in all of the turmoil of the world, everything that occurs to our conditioned mind as *serious*, as *not play*, as cause for termination of the game, and we allow its heat to purify our body and mind. We transmute the challenges of the game, including those challenges that go far off script, into gifts. For we know that, without them, we could never attain those heights we aspire to. We allow our rage to pierce us to the core, our grief to saturate our bones, and learn to appreciate the textures and feeling tones of every one of these emotions, including the ones we would otherwise reflexively avoid, suppress, or withdraw from. We allow our gameboard to continually expand to include more of us, including the externalizations of those parts we feel other than, such as violators and their manipulations, their physical and emotional violence. We take in all of it, and we do so lightly, with the awareness that *this is play*.

5

On Covert Games,
or Unveiling the Infinite

Though we seem to be sleeping, there is an inner wakefulness that directs the
dream, and will eventually startle us back to the truth of who we are.[1]

—RUMI

There is no doubt that the Game has its dangers. For that very reason we love
it; only the weak are sent out on paths without perils. But never forget what I
have told you so often: our mission is to recognize contraries for what they are:
first of all as contraries, but then as opposite poles of a unity.[2]

—MAGISTER LUDI, A CHARACTER IN
HERMANN HESSE'S *THE GLASS BEAD GAME*

A HALLUCINATED PLAYGROUND

We saw that the Lila myth treats the universe as a cosmic game of
hide-and-seek, in which the god of play conceals himself in every crevice
of creation, forgets that he is playing a game, forgets that he has forgotten, and forgets even that he is a god. Not satisfied with limiting himself
to the pristine, orderly dimensions of experience, the god of play wants
to know what it is to ache, to yearn, to tremble, and to be stretched to the
outermost limits of his being. He wants to know the whole of life, from
the despairing convalescence of the invalid's illness to the spellbound

rapture of the lover's yearning, the perfect stillness of the Benedictine's prayer to the sweat-drenched agony of the soldier's nightmare.

So, he dreams the world into being, conjuring it out of nothingness as a playground for his amusement. One Lila myth conveys this dream-like nature of our reality by depicting the Lord of the Universe asleep "on a cosmic serpent . . . in the middle of the primordial ocean," before the dawn of creation. "During his sleep a lotus grows from his naval and the demiurge is created, who in turn creates the world."[3]

The Buddha—a name that translates as "the awakened one," echoes this perception when he tells us "how to contemplate our conditioned existence in this fleeting world: like a tiny drop of dew, or a bubble floating in a stream; like a flash of lightning in a summer cloud, or a flickering lamp, an illusion, a phantom, a dream."[4]

The mystical poet Rumi takes this one step further when he tells us that "there is an inner wakefulness that directs the dream, and will eventually startle us back to the truth of who we are."[5] This inner wakefulness is what the Buddhists call our Buddha nature, that indestructible quality of awareness that operates underneath the various layers of conditioned identity—of who we think we are and how we think we ought to act based on the time, place, culture, and social position we were born into.

However deep we may descend into this conditioning, there is an inner wakefulness that directs the dream, guiding us at every turn in the game. This inner wakefulness is our divinity as it's used in this chapter's context: It is the part of us that chose to enter this life and experience these sets of circumstances for its play.

In the vast imagination of the cosmic creator, each individual life constitutes a world of its own, dreamed up out of his or her desire to play with and know the full spectrum of experience. Entering such a world, we obscure our true, divine nature and acculturate ourselves to the implicit rules, goals, and constraints that we find. From there, the hidden God in each of us begins to seek its own reflection in every other part of the universe, wanting only to remember its own divinity by witnessing that divinity in others.

This forgetting of our true nature, this descent into the dream world we take seriously, sets the context in which the covert games of our lives take place. We saw that every game occurs on a physical or mental field of play and is defined by the same four elements: a set of rules; a goal; a feedback system; and voluntary participation. Each of these elements is equally present in a covert game as they are in an overt game. The only difference is that a covert game conceals this structure, whereas an overt game reveals it.

Consider the difference between the elements, rules, and objectives in football versus a woman trying to get a man's attention at a party. Her goal is no less clear to her than the football player's is to him. And the rules that structure her pursuit of that goal are just as clear to her as to any overt game player. She knows she can glance in his direction, however subtly, but that she absolutely should not take her shirt off. The social cost of the latter infraction would be much higher than any foul penalty in an overt game. And that's just as obvious to her, and to everyone around her, as the rules of football are to its players and spectators.

Just like an overt game player, her attention is constantly alert for feedback, for any indication that she has successfully drawn his attention. She looks for a bead of sweat to drop down the back of his neck as eagerly as any chess master hunts for a check against an opponent. With no less sophistication, she seeks to corner him, to capture him, to nail him to the ground so that he can hardly move a millimeter, only to draw him in so magnetically that he can't resist approaching her.

Intuitively, we all know this. Of this hidden game, we may first be aware of our culture's implicit rules—rules that tell us how we can and cannot dress, speak, make love, and establish our livelihoods.

Analyzing the particular obstacles and restrictions around us may reveal our deeper, psychological games, which in turn have their roots in the family system we grew up in and the types of interpersonal play we learned from our parents, themselves players in the game we find ourselves born into. The psychotherapist Eric Berne speaks to this when he refers to "child rearing . . . [as] an educational process in which the child is taught what [covert] games to play and how to play them. . . . The favored game of any individual can be traced back to their parents and grandparents, and forward to their children. . . . Different cultures and different social classes favor different types of games, and various tribes and families favor different variations of these."[6]

Although the structure of these activities may appear quite different from that of a formal game, even video game designers are beginning to structure their experiences in this way. "It used to be that we were spoon-fed the goal and the rules," writes McGonigal, "and we would then seek feedback on our progress. But increasingly, the feedback systems are what we learn first. They guide us toward the goal and help us decode the rules. And that's as powerful a motivation to play as any: Discovering exactly what is possible in this brand-new virtual world."[7]

And so it is with the cosmic game: We throw ourselves into a dream world, into a hallucinated playground, and learn to discern its rules and goals from the feedback we receive along the way. Some of this feedback we receive overtly (we set the fork on *this* side of the plate). But most of it we absorb implicitly, through trial and error, and through the messaging we assimilate—from the media we consume, the peers with whom we associate, and a whole constellation of other avenues through which we learn to constrain our behavior to play along well with others.

Rather than feel trapped within these games, we may choose skillful ways of relating to them. For the feedback we receive, at one level, tells us how to move toward the goals implicit in these covert games. But, at another level, this feedback can alert us to the contours of the game itself—letting us know precisely what kind of game we're in, and what the fact of our having chosen that game as opposed to another might tell us about our consciousness, including its deeper recesses of which we may not be aware. The first recognition of a covert game may challenge our concept of voluntary participation until we acknowledge the subconscious desires of our psyche and the elements of ourselves that we may liberate and fulfill by our participation in the play. In discovering the workings of this game, we may uncover the forgotten moment, years or even lifetimes ago when we chose to participate in this game and finally again encounter the ever-present choice of whether we will continue to play. Freedoms that we would otherwise never recognize become revealed as equal options to us.

In time, as we discover exactly what is possible in this world, we may find that some of its rules are meant to be broken, and some of its goals are better off ignored. For beneath the surface-level covert games we're guided toward by our environment, an infinite game awaits in which enemies are friends, violation is a gift, boundaries are porous, and rules can be rewritten in the course of play. To move into this deeper game is to awaken to our divinity and to allow its expression to pour out into the world.

RESONANCE AND ATTRACTION

These are the games we have become accustomed to like a fish to water. They define the landscape of our internal cognitive map, charted from the very beginnings of our engagement with the environment around us. Consider the vulnerability with which our soul chooses to enter into this world: When we first emerge from the watery bliss of uterine containment and enter the differentiated world of light and sound, we are at once confronted with the helplessness and dependency inherent to mammalian life on Earth. Absent the regulating effect of our parents, and in particular our mother, we would die within a few days after birth, even if provided with adequate food and clothing. Such is the importance of connection, relationship, and intimacy to the development of the Self—of who we are as living, breathing, feeling beings in this world. Our mother will act as the original "other" of our lives, and the quality of her attention, as well as her emotional availability and the steadiness of her nervous system, will imprint our initial sense of how safe life will or won't feel. That feeling of safety, along with feelings of social closeness and other emotions are regulated by the limbic system that assimilates the undifferentiated cues and sensations of the outside to provide the reciprocal sense of internal well-being.

In these first few years of heightened neurological flexibility, our primary relationships lay down the formative tracks that direct the development of our psychic and neural architecture, giving focus to our wide-open potential. These tracks, known as *limbic attractors*, form the neural constraints on the interpretations we will use to color our experiences—the map by which we navigate the world and the lens through which we see it. The psychological phenomenon of transference describes the process by which we project aspects of our early childhood relationships onto the people we come into contact with, and then emotionally react to them as though they were people from our past, distorted by the effect of these limbic attractors. They encourage us to read into our interpretations consistent with the scripts we wrote in childhood, even if those interpretations conflict with the underlying facts of the situation.

For example, a man who felt too rigidly controlled in his childhood may later come to see, in his girlfriend's request for him to put away the dishes, evidence that she is trying to control, manipulate, and micromanage him, just as his mother did. And the girlfriend, raised by a father who did not allow her to speak up and advocate for her needs, might see, in her boyfriend's angry reaction to her quite reasonable requests, evidence that it is not safe for her to express her wants, needs, and desires in her relationships. However kindly she might ask him not to leave the sink full of dirty dishes overnight, he would likely still react with angry defensiveness, a response to a pattern embedded in his psyche. Neither of them will be in touch with the underlying facts of the situation, as both will be too preoccupied with reenacting the painful conflicts of their past.

And, wherever possible, we will attract dynamics whose facts *do* indeed map the contours of our scripts. The evidence produced reinforces our certainty of how the world is and, on a certain level, our mind feels rewarded for accurately predicting the outcome. Our limbic systems then are continually transmitting invitations for others to synchronize with our emotional rhythms, and they have a tendency to attract players whose formative imprints complement our own. "Limbic attractors thus exert a distorting force not only within the brain that produces them," write three psychiatrists in *A General Theory of Love*, "but also on the limbic networks of others—calling forth compatible memories, emotional states, and styles of relatedness in them."[8]

The apparent magnetism with which we attract experiences consistent with our childhood conflicts is rooted in the biological reality of our limbic systems. "The young man with a fondness for faultfinding lovers is [therefore] in even more trouble than he thinks. First, he must contend with the mental mechanism that leads him with uncanny precision to a woman who is herself critical. Second, his presence will magnify whatever minatory tendencies his current paramour may possess."[9] The ultimate goal of the covert game may then be to simply become aware of the play we find ourselves immersed within.

BEHIND THE VEIL

To the extent that we are carrying the emotional baggage of our past and performing a script that originated there, we are alienated from our true nature, as well as the true nature of others. We react to life in a stereotyped fashion as we project these childhood conflicts onto the people around us and insist they play a role in our drama. When we live theatrically, that is, we stop seeing others as unique human beings and begin to see them as abstractions.

To see someone as an abstraction, to interact with them as a role rather than as a person, is to rob them of their humanity. When we see that woman as "wife," that man as "lawyer," and that child as "illegal immigrant," we treat these individuals as types rather than as human beings with unique stories of their own. We reduce them to objects that must be manipulated to play a part, rather than as autonomous, thinking, feeling beings. Disregarding this autonomy, we obscure the quality of perception that would allow us to see intimately into the yearnings, woundings, and intentions of the other. The psychoanalyst Jessica Benjamin refers to the resulting dynamic as a do-er and done-to relationship, "in which the dominant form is coercion or submission, in which action and response are not freely given." The irony is that "each person may feel coerced by the other, as if pushed into their assigned role, neither in control."[10] When we "collapse into two-ness" in this way—to use Benjamin's term—we feel as though the other is responsible for our pain, and that the only way to find relief is to forcibly change the other's behavior. In time, these do-er and done-to relationships tend to magnetize a third position: that of the would-be mediator, or rescuer. Even as the rescuer may appear to be helping, this player reinforces the abstractness of the other two players by relating to them as their roles rather than as the individuals beneath these roles. The ensuing dynamic of victim, persecutor, and rescuer—known as the *victim triangle*—is the mental field upon which all covert games take place.

Spiritual teacher Lynne Forrest has found that, although we typically move through all three positions on the triangle during a covert game, we are predisposed to initiating these games from the one position that corresponds most closely to our childhood imprints. Lynne refers to these as *starting-gate positions.* Someone who witnessed violence in their childhood, for instance, might later take on the role of rescuer as a starting-gate position, sensing a personal responsibility to restore order. Someone who learned that being sad or hurt was the best way to receive attention may habitually take on the role of "victim." The persecutor role may be taken on by someone who has experienced a childhood of uncertainty and later adopted a survival mindset, committed to "getting theirs" before anyone might take advantage of them.

These roles we take on for ourselves set the ways in which we see the world and everyone in it according to the role they serve, relative to ours. When our self-projections happen to line up with another's, we bond in the prearranged ways: the intractably antagonistic cycle of blame and misunderstanding between rescuer and persecutor, the codependent marriage between a rescuer and victim, or even the abusive relationship between a persecutor and victim. "Why would they stay?" we ask, but it is the mesmerizing comfort of familiarity that draws us deeper into our roles. We enact familiar, proven scenes to generate their predictable results, which we take as evidence to reinforce our belief of who we are and how the world works. Like a prized trophy, we will compete with others to prove that we are the "most victim" or "most persecutor," flashing our evidence or, in arguments, aggressively forcing others back into the roles we have assigned to them. That force exerted by a victim to convince her perceived "persecutor" of his fault or compel her "rescuer" of his responsibility may then, ironically, feel to those projected on as persecution, instigating layers of interrelated drama, echoing like a hall of mirrors. We live within these restricted, isolated dramas, purposefully blind to the impact we have on the humans living beneath the roles we have projected onto them. We live far from the intimacy of play, bristling at any threat to disturb the fixed reality within our bubble.

THE CENTRAL PARADOX OF THESE dramatic dynamics—first alluded to by James Carse—is that we can only play a position on the triangle by forgetting that we have chosen to do so. This doesn't mean that we don't genuinely experience suffering and aren't victimized by others. But there is a distinction between *being victimized* and taking on the *identity of a victim:* The former is a matter of what happened to us; the latter, to paraphrase physician and trauma expert Gabor Maté, is a matter of what we decided about ourselves and the world, based on what happened to us.

Compared to the decorative glory of overt competition, covert games occur at the level of identity. With each instance of play, we aim to assert or maintain our preferred identity, expeditiously relegating our challengers to their assigned roles. To acknowledge our participation in this game would be to recognize our volition in continuing the play as well as the option to take on an identity outside our preference—or to even step entirely outside the restricted positions of the triangle itself.

THE THEATER OF CONSCIOUSNESS

Recall that the Sanskrit word "Lila" translates as both the verb and the noun form of "play," suggesting that every moment of existence is a theatrical performance, a dramatic scene in the dynamic play of life. In the last section, we saw how the simple dynamics of fixed roles and relationships can project entire trajectories of drama, writing the scripts we feel compelled to enact. The life scripts of this theater bind even the most disparate players into overlapping narratives, creating shared worlds of meaning that constrain, contain, and contextualize the various covert games of our lives. To unravel the mystery of these games, then, we must first understand the scripted worlds they're bound within.

In his 1961 book *Transactional Analysis in Psychotherapy*, Eric Berne writes that covert "games tend to be segments of larger, more complex sets of transactions called scripts." He locates the origins of these scripts in the "infantile reactions and experiences" from childhood that we later project onto those around us, in order to re-create the dramas of our upbringing.[11] For example, a woman raised by an absent father might find herself unconsciously drawn to emotionally unavailable men who abandon her at the climax of their relationship. She may find herself drawn, as if by magnetism, to men with complementary scripts ("women are needy and inhibit my freedom"), playing out a predictable series of scenes that move inevitably toward abandonment. She might then seek the consolation of other women with similar scripts ("I told you men were good for nothing!") to both comfort her and reinforce her narrative.

As a child, she may have received messaging from her mother that men were emotionally unavailable and would leave her eventually, just as her father did. The combination of her early childhood wounding, resulting from her father's absence, and the messaging she received from her mother, which verbalized and concretized her pain into a core statement ("men will leave when things get hard"), crystallizes into a life script that she then plays out for many years after the original conflict.

These core statements—formed in early childhood conflicts, during which we internalized a primal image of what life was and could be—are the knots from which we weave the fabric of our lives together. Our formative experiences communicate to us, first viscerally and later verbally, what love feels like, how relations operate, and what to expect from the world. They introduce the nuclear dynamics that will ripple out into our lives, taking the form of those baffling synchronicities, those repetitive scenarios, that feeling of dating the same person over and over in so many different bodies.

IF IT WEREN'T FOR YOU

Now that we've established the context in which life's dramatic scenes play out, let's take a closer look at what makes these dramas a form of gameplay. In his book *Games People Play,* Berne introduces us to a woman named Mrs. White whose favorite pastime is to complain (victim) about her controlling husband (persecutor). Her biggest complaint is that he refuses to let her sign up for a dance class. She tells us that, if it weren't for him, she would be living out her dream as a professional dancer by now. Instead, she must resign herself to the dreary life of a domestic housewife.

After several years of thwarted desire, Mrs. White begins to see a therapist, who helps her examine her options and motives, instead of remaining externally focused on her husband and his supposed flaws. A few short weeks of this self-inquiry helps her gather up the courage to go to a dance class—to hell with what her husband might have to say about it! Upon arriving at the class, she discovers, to her horror, that she is terrified of dancing and has been all along.[12]

In his analysis of the game, Berne points out that, "out of her many suitors, she had picked a domineering man for a husband. She was then in a position to complain that she could do all sorts of things 'if it weren't for you.' Many of her woman friends also had domineering husbands, and when they met for their morning coffee, they spent a good deal of time playing 'if it weren't for him.' . . . As it turned out, however, contrary to her complaints, her husband was performing a very real service for her by forbidding her to do something she was deeply afraid of, and by preventing her, in fact, from even becoming aware of her fears."[13]

In other words, by freely assuming the victim role, Mrs. White had been able to obscure the covert benefits she was deriving from her husband's behavior—such as the opportunity to avoid her fear of dancing, and the opportunity to have something to complain about to her friends. Mr. White, for his part, had also obscured the truth of their relationship by assuming the persecutor role. This allowed him to hide, from himself and others, the power his wife covertly wielded in the relationship—namely, the power to coerce him into "dominating" her, so that she could then blame him for her voluntary problems.

True, she may not have had to work very hard to elicit this behavior. But the very fact that she had been benefiting from, if not encouraging or even directing her own oppression, speaks to the inherent ambiguity of a covert game—an ambiguity that is neatly reduced out of existence by the theatricality of its roles. This is why the rescuer role, played by Mrs. White's friends, is so essential: By colluding against her husband, they reinforce the theatricality of the dynamic—no doubt with the expectation that Mrs. White would collude against *their* husbands when the time came.

RULES

So, what is it that makes this a game? With what justification can we use the same word to describe a covert game like "if it weren't for you" as we use to describe an overt game like chess or basketball?

We saw that every game takes place on a physical and mental field of play. In the case of "if it weren't for you," the physical field includes Mr. and Mrs. White's home, the women's favorite coffee shop, and any other physical spaces in which the players assumed their scripted roles in pursuit of a covert goal. And the mental field includes the core beliefs from which the players generate these scripts in the first place, as well as the limbic attractors they use to cast the drama, and the various smokescreens they use to conceal its voluntary nature.

Let's take a closer look at each of the elements in the context of these covert games.

Every covert game is contained by a set of implicit rules or boundaries. Although unstated, these boundaries are no less immutable than those of an overt game. They limit what the players can and cannot do with each other in their play. In doing so, they create a reality internal to the game—a world with its own rules, roles, and aims. To say that a covert game occurs within a world is to acknowledge that its players have collectively constructed a bounded reality in which to realize their overlapping aims. For the rules codify, albeit implicitly, the shared values and complementary goals that the players have gathered to pursue.

Consider that Mrs. White's game of "if it weren't for you" ended the moment she made an off-script play and freely went to that dance class, without continuing to pretend that her husband had the power to stop her. By violating the implicit rules of the game, she ended its play abruptly. For how could she continue to play the victim after the covert benefits of doing so had been unveiled for all to see? Just as a soccer player could not continue his game after leaving its physical field of play, Mrs. White could not continue her game by leaving its mental field of play—by acknowledging her fears and her complicity in her "oppression."

There is, however, a cost to this crossing of boundaries: To leave the world of the game would be to risk abandonment from its associated friend group, which would no longer be able to involve us in their favorite games. This is why, as Berne notes, "people pick as friends, associates, and intimates other people who play the same games. Hence 'everybody who is anybody' in a given social circle (upper-class society, juvenile gang, social club, college campus, etc.) behaves in a way that might seem quite foreign to members of a different social circle. Conversely, any member of a social circle who changes his game will tend to be extruded but will find himself welcome at some other social circle."[14]

This social reinforcement of the implicit rules of play is what holds the bounded world of a covert game together. Despite the fluid nature of social reality, the incredible complexity of relationships, and the freedom of players to travel an arbitrarily large physical arena, these games remain coherent and cohered due to each player's voluntary upholding of its agreed-upon boundaries.

GOAL

The game structure of these activities becomes clearer when we consider the goals, or payoffs, that the players are playing for. The psychologist Stephen Karpman defines this payoff as "what 'happens' at the end of the triangle dance—but is secretly the purpose of the game."[15] Just as the opening moves of a chess match are meant to set up for a checkmate, the opening moves of a covert game are meant to "set up . . . for this payoff . . . but they are always designed to harvest the maximum permissible satisfaction at each step."[16] Here, too, the parallel applies: for the game of chess, like any other formal game, is likewise designed so that each step toward the goal is a source of exhilaration.

Most covert games are played to reinforce an old belief system, originating in childhood.[17] The preliminary moves of these games are therefore designed to elicit the emotional and physiological states we associate with those beliefs. Perhaps Mrs. White, for example, was shamed as a child for pursuing her desires, and so concluded that her desires were shameful and bad. One way to reinforce this belief system as an adult would be to attract a husband who would criticize her for wanting things—in this case, to go to a dance class. The painful feelings of anger, resentment, and helplessness she would collect during their relationship would signal to her that *she had succeeded* in finding a husband who would confirm her script by playing her favorite games with her.

Their implicit agreement might look something like this: He would help her luxuriate in the edgy taboo of feeling totally controlled, shamed, and dominated. And she would help him delight in the playful amplification of his power, in the illusion of controlling, of all things, feminine desire—the force that even the Biblical God himself could not arrest in the garden.

Under the veil of victimhood, she would ask him to be the face of her own power, and he would ask her to be the face of his own helplessness. In this projection dance, the two could then move slowly toward intimacy with that which they had discarded in themselves—namely, Mrs. White's agency and Mr. White's helplessness. From this perspective, the generosity of their partnership becomes apparent. For the two could only come to know these hidden parts of themselves through the dark side of the other.

FEEDBACK SYSTEM

Every move in a covert game, then, must be understood at two simultaneous levels of abstraction. At the social level, our moves fulfill the expectations of our peer groups and reinforce our performed roles of victim, persecutor, and rescuer; at the limbic level, our moves communicate a symphony of emotional tones, orchestrating our movements and directing us with exacting precision toward the affirmation of our core beliefs.

The feedback system of a covert game takes place at this second, limbic level, and begins always with an invitation to play. This may be nonverbal, such as "turning a cold shoulder, batting a flirty eye, shaking an accusative finger, tracking mud in the house, [or] reading someone's mail."[18] If the other player accepts our invitation by, for example, scolding us for tracking mud in the house, then we can be sure that we are well on our way to fulfilling our goal. The taboo feelings that our playmate elicits in us along the way—such as shame, anger, humiliation, or indignation—will then alert us to how effectively we are moving toward this goal. By reminding us of our childhood conflicts, these feelings let us know that we will soon be confirming our core beliefs at the climax of the game.

Every time Jenny pops a Xanax, for example, she fulfills two contradictory purposes at once: She numbs the painful feelings of her childhood, while inviting Tommy to re-create those feelings by treating her as a broken victim that can only be loved by being fixed. In the topsy-turvy logic of a covert game, these invitations to play even the most destructive dynamics are meant to create a sense of safety and stability. They bring order to the world, and thus to our consciousness, by proving to us that our map of the world corresponds to the territory of our reality—however disordered that reality may be.

Gabor and his son Daniel Maté illustrate this principle through the case of Leslie, a forty-year-old woman who had attempted suicide more than a dozen times. In *The Myth of Normal: Trauma, Illness, and Healing in a Toxic Culture,* they tell us that undergoing a healing process of compassionate self-reflection, Leslie came to see that her self-harming behaviors "'were actually trying to protect me from the deep pain that I was trying not to feel.' . . . These [behaviors] included hitting herself with a leather belt, as her mother had done when Leslie was a child. When I asked her what that did for her, she answered: 'it would kind of calm me down a bit. I would be *less dysregulated.*' Surprising but true: the very mental patterns and behaviors that seem to throw our lives into such chaos originate as an attempt, a temporary and partially effective one . . . to bring our bodies and minds into equilibrium."[19]

VOLUNTARY PARTICIPATION

Few of us would care to admit that this kind of suffering might be voluntary, that we have freely cocreated so much agony in our lives— the same agony we have spent so long feeling victimized by. Nearly every inner inclination revolts at the idea of personal responsibility in these matters. Not only is it humiliating to acknowledge our part in life's challenges; it is also a sure path to disqualification from one or another covert game, rejection from its peer group, and exposure to the feelings we had used that game to deny.

This resistance is not only personal, but collective as well. For the fabric of our society, whose seams are held together by the many covert games it's built to organize, resists with every rule and norm and custom the exposure of our freedom to depart—let alone our eagerness to stay within—the bounded worlds created by our voluntary games.

Such an exposure, then, can only be moved toward indirectly.

We can start by seeking to understand the players' hidden motives— the payoffs or goals toward which their moves are oriented. We might then discover that, just like Mrs. White, their covert games provide them with excellent opportunities to pursue these goals. Or, we might consider that these games terminate the moment any player steps outside the scripted role and performs a countermove that contradicts the other player's ability to continue the game. We might then discover that all other players are similarly free to make an off-script play at any moment, and have simply chosen otherwise, to pursue their goals within the game. These players, rightly offended, will often shun the unveiled other. But in the moment of unveiling, it becomes clear that each of them—at least in principle—have the power to set down their scripted role and enter into real intimacy with each other instead.

Consider the case of Lois Wilson, wife of a raging alcoholic named Bill, who would eventually find sobriety and become the founder of Alcoholics Anonymous.

"My one purpose in life was to help him get over this terrible habit," she writes. "Together we tried everything we could think of. . . . During two successive summers I gave up my job, and we escaped for three months to the country for renewal and rebuilding. Nothing worked. *I had to assume family responsibilities and make all decisions. . . .*

"Bill did nothing but drink. He was afraid to leave the house for fear the police would pick him up. We lived entirely to ourselves. We had dropped all our friends or been dropped by them and we saw as little of our families as possible. Our whole life had simmered down to one terrified fight against alcohol. It was tragic indeed to watch such a fine man become completely beaten and hopeless."[20]

No matter how hard Lois tried to rescue Bill from his alcoholism, things continued to spiral out of control. As Bill describes it:

"The house was taken over by the mortgage holder, my mother-in-law died, my wife and father-in-law became ill. . . . Sometimes I stole from my wife's slender purse when the morning terror and madness were on me. . . . Then came the night when the physical and mental torture was so hellish I feared I would burst through my window. . . . I managed to drag my mattress to a lower floor, lest I suddenly leap. . . . People feared for my sanity. . . . So did I. . . . She would soon have to give me over to the undertaker or the asylum."[21]

After years spent desperately trying to rescue Bill from this condition, a miracle happened: An old drinking buddy of Bill's called him, let him know that he was sober, and asked if they could get together to talk. During this meeting, his friend convinced Bill to quit drinking and gave him a pathway toward continued sobriety.

The path worked. From that day on, to the day he died, Bill never touched another drink.

"Bill figured that since a miracle had happened to him and his friend it could happen to others, so he worked endlessly and tirelessly to help alcoholics," Lois writes. "After a while I began to wonder why I was not as happy as I ought to be, since the one thing I had been yearning for all my married life had come to pass. Then one Sunday, Bill asked me if I was ready to go to the [AA] meeting with him. To my own astonishment as well as his, I burst forth with, 'damn your old meetings!' and threw a shoe as hard as I could."[22]

This shocking scene led Lois to a discovery: On the surface, she had desperately wanted Bill to recover from his alcoholism, but on the deeper, limbic level, she was getting a hefty payoff from his descent into hell. When Bill made a countermove that brought their covert game to an end, and so robbed her of her favorite pastime, she naturally reacted with rage and aggression.

"This surprise display of temper over nothing pulled me up short and made me start to analyze my own attitudes," she writes. "By degrees I saw that I had been wallowing in self-pity, that I resented the fact that Bill and I never spent any time together anymore, and that I was left alone while he was off somewhere scouting new drunks or working with old ones. I felt on the outside of a very tight little clique of alcoholics that no mere wife could enter. My pride was hurt by the fact that a friend, another alcoholic, had been able to do for Bill in a short time what I had tried and failed to do all our married years."[23]

"My life's purpose of sobering up Bill, *what had made me feel desperately needed,* had vanished. I sought something to fill the void. As I began to be honest with myself, I recognized how greatly Bill had developed spiritually. . . . I decided to strive for my own spiritual growth. I used the same principles as he did to learn how to change my attitudes."[24]

THE INTIMACY OF UNVEILING

Unlike overt games, which make use of external obstacles and goals to draw forth what is within us, the objective of our participation in covert games is most often for our participation and its incentives to remain concealed so that we may continue our under-the-radar play. Rather than unveiling the vulnerability of our desires, we obscure them from ourselves and others and move toward their fulfillment indirectly. True intimacy with our external playmates is therefore not possible within the boundaries of a covert game. But this is not to demonize or devalue our covert games. If we consider these games within the larger context of the cosmic game, we can see that this intimacy avoidance itself serves a crucial purpose. For we did not descend into the dreamworld of this life to view it from a distance, but rather to saturate ourselves entirely in the full range of experiences it has to offer—to gain intimacy with the darker, more painful, more constricting experiences just as much as the lighter, more buoyant experiences.

These darker experiences can only be known through the vehicle of a covert game, pulling us further inward. Paradoxically, these games draw us deeper into life by allowing us to become intimate with the emotional textures that can only be known by distance—from hunger to desperation, suffering to loneliness, manipulation to confusion, insecurity to despair.

These emotional experiences are not to be discounted. As Mo Gawdat, formerly of Google X, commented to Peter Diamandis of Singularity University on the possibility that our entire existence may be a simulation: "What's the answer to a challenging game? To play, to fully engage, to be a part of it! It doesn't matter if it's a simulation or if it's real life."[25] Despite the nature of our circumstances, even in the most remote and bleak scenarios, the option for play exists as the medium of liberation, the path toward intimacy with all of existence.

THE ENEMY'S GIFT

The dramatic scenes of our lives, and the covert games that play out within them, are therefore best understood as increasingly advanced arenas of play. To paraphrase Carl Jung, they draw us into those conditions of "inner necessity" from which the "play instinct" can create "something new."[26] The enemy's gift draws us into these conditions. Although the forms of these enemies are varied—appearing now as a terminal illness or unexpected divorce, now as the loss of a cherished job or the death of a loved one—they all share the same purpose: to startle us back to the truth of who we are. With the devotion of a lover, the enemies of our lives drive us mercilessly into the most charged and treacherous dimensions of the psyche, squeezing our mind and pressing its contents up to the surface of our awareness. They know that our mastery and freedom can only rise in proportion to the conditions that life throws at us, to cultivate the flexibility to meet our obstacles with love. And they know this flexibility can only be attained by the removal of its impediments—those inner obstacles to free play—which take the form of long-buried beliefs, suppressed emotions, painful experiences from our past, and the decisions we made about ourselves and the world as a result of those experiences.

The playwright and cancer survivor formerly known as Eve Ensler (who now refers to herself as "V") speaks to this when she asks, what if "when you got sick, you weren't a stage [of a disease] but in a process? And cancer, just like having your heart broken, or getting a new job, or going to school, were a teacher? What if, rather than being cast out and defined by some terminal category, you were identified as someone in the middle of a transformation that could deepen your soul, open your heart?"[27]

Gabor and Daniel Maté remind us of the optionality that is still present in the inextricable situation of our lives by suggesting that "if disease is a manifestation of something in our lives rather than merely their cruel disruptor, we have options: we can pursue new understandings, ask new questions, perhaps make new choices. We can take our rightful place as active participants in the process, rather than remain its victims. . . . It may not be the guest we ever desire to see, but a modicum of hospitality—welcoming the unwelcome, so to speak—costs us nothing. It may even lead to an opportunity to find out why this particular visitor has come to call, and what it might tell us about our lives."[28]

When we remember Nachmanovitch's insight that "each episode of our life reflects our own mind back at us, complete with all its imperfections, exactly as it is," we can see these enemies for what they truly are—our inner guides. They are the ones willing to drive us into a concentrated exploration of our true nature, beneath the masks we present to the world. For the conflicts they draw us into reflect back to us, in perfect detail, the formative experiences of our childhood, as well as the emotional knots that we formed around those experiences.

To draw us into contact with these knots—which take the form of early wounds, crystallized into core statements about reality—is to present us with the opportunity to untie them. If we are willing to revision our enemies as guides instead of antagonists, we can allow them to draw us into that liminal space of re-creation, in which we can reconsider and rewrite our reality.

Jung described this process as a movement through "a tight passage, a narrow door, whose painful constriction no one is spared who goes down to the deep well. But . . . after the door is, surprisingly enough, no above and no below, no here and no there, no mine and no thine, no good and no bad. It is the world . . . where I am indivisibly this and that; where I experience the other in myself and the other-than-myself experiences me."[29]

Unlike the opponents of an overt game, these enemies—and the initiations they summon us toward—cannot be outrun. Wherever we go, there they will be, mirroring back to us with perfect faithfulness the contents of our scripts. Because our limbic attractors are continually calling them into our field of play, we can move from London to Madagascar, and we'll still find them there, awaiting us and ready to play the same role—just with a different face, and perhaps in a different language. And just like Waitzkin's Russian chess rival, they'll be perfectly content to escalate the dynamic until we turn and face them—or, more precisely, turn and face the inner aspects of ourselves they are reflecting.

For example, if our mother was always too busy for us when we were growing up, then our enemies might take the form of a therapist who always shows up late for our appointments (persecutor). Perhaps we will choose to collude against her with our (rescuer) friends, as "if it weren't for her" lateness, we would be "fixed" by now (victim). In time, we may leave this therapist and resent her for not having been able to rehabilitate us more effectively. Seeking a fresh start, we might then move to

Paris and fall in love with a charming Parisian man, only to be abandoned by him on our wedding day. Devastated and no one to whom we can turn to process our emotions, we might then internalize our grief and develop a mysterious chronic illness. This would allow us to bounce around from one doctor to another and resent them all for their inability to repair us. We would surely have recovered years ago "if it weren't for them," but due to our doctors' inability to help, we become increasingly convalescent. Eventually, we decide to hire an in-home nurse to take care of us. And the nurse, for her part, occasionally forgets to show up for work—coincidentally on precisely those days when we need her the most.

UNTYING THE KNOTS

Each successive round of a game like this presents a firmer invitation to reconsider our early decisions about reality and make the movement from scriptedness to unscriptedness. But, given the tendency of our scripts to compel us toward role-bound reactions to our experiences, how can we make such a move?

The process is simple, but not easy: We begin with the recognition that, just by virtue of being born, we have been thrown into a world with a finite script, choreographed by our formative experiences with our family and our larger social environment. Only by admitting that we have been compulsively performing a scripted life plan, and participating in the various covert games that structure the scenes within that script, can we begin to understand the precise nature of the overlays we have been placing onto reality. We acknowledge that we are—and always have been—situated in a scripted world, and we decide to get to know that world on its own terms.

We then decide to take all of our life experiences as feedback, alerting us to the precise qualities of our script. In taking the episodes of our lives as reflections of our minds, rather than as affronts to our happiness, we can begin to uncouple our projected narrative from the underlying reality. Instead of reflexively reacting to events with the same scripted behavior as always, we can insert a pause between stimulus and response, during which we can ask ourselves questions like, "What is this experience telling me about my own mind?" rather than questions like, "What is this experience telling me about how awful and fundamentally unfair life is?" In other words, we can begin to examine our scripts, rather than merely perform our scripts.

Psychologists refer to this skill as *cognitive reappraisal*. Simply put, it means considering alternative interpretations to what we're experiencing in the moment. Take the case of anxiety: McGonigal notes that, physiologically, anxiety and excitement are "the exact same emotion. Whether you're anxious about something or excited about it, your body responds in a nearly identical 'high arousal' state. You have excess energy, you may feel butterflies in your stomach, your heart rate may increase, and so on. This means that when you're feeling anxious about a problem, it's much easier to try to get excited about solving it than try to calm it down. . . . You just have to change how your mind interprets what you're feeling."[30]

Cognitive reappraisal gives us the freedom to try out different ways of relating to an experience. We enter into the space between scriptedness and unscriptedness, the known and the unknown, and stay right there in the groundlessness of that location. We set down our preconceptions about reality, our ready-made interpretations of what's happening in the moment, and we enter into a place of not knowing. We confess that we simply don't know the limits on how much responsibility we can take for our experience. We don't know exactly how we might have orchestrated this scene. We don't know the payoffs we have been playing for, or how those payoffs might overlap with those of our apparent enemies. We don't even know the limits on the types of questions we can ask in this exploration.

All we know is that we have become willing to enter into the gray area between narrative and reality and question every taken-for-granted "fact" and justification we encounter there. We have decided to treat the boundaries of our scripted world as permeable, and to entertain the possibility that, with enough courage, we just might be able to walk straight through those boundaries. Having come to believe that "the joy we get from living," in Csikszentmihalyi's words, "ultimately depends directly on how the mind filters and interprets experience," we determine to get to know our filters as intimately as possible.[31] And we recognize that the best way to do so is to study the reflections provided by the enemies of our lives: the illnesses that have plagued us, the friends that have betrayed us, the opportunities of which we were robbed, the lovers who have broken our hearts.

For we can be sure that, the moment we feel done-to by another, we are engaged in a projection. We can then choose to doubt the solidity of these projections by recognizing them for what they are: externalized aspects of our interior landscapes. Instead of holding our enemies responsible for these projections, we can choose to turn within—toward the painful constriction of that narrow doorway—and seek there the primordial roots of our conflicts. Like unraveling the threads of an ancient tapestry, we can follow our feelings down into the underlying thoughts that give rise to them. And as we follow these threads back to their origins, we can begin to intuit what Waitzkin calls the "hidden harmonies" beneath the surface chaos of our lives—the deeper order in which our turbulent dramas are elegantly contained.

This alternating movement from feeling to thought, and thought to feeling, will eventually lead us to a central knot—the primal belief we formed in early childhood and have been enacting ever since. To arrive at this knot is to arrive at the freedom to choose: whether to allow this belief to continue to entangle us, or to leave behind its scripted world and walk straight into infinity.

In her book *Guiding Principles for Life Beyond Victim Consciousness*, Lynne Forrest concisely outlines what this process might look like. Let's apply a summary of her method to the drama of the absent nurse and see where it might take us.

The next time the nurse forgets to show up to our house, we can insert a space between this stimulus and our response. Instead of performing the same old, predictable outrage, we can turn inward and face our feelings with curiosity. If we're feeling outrage, we can ask ourselves what thought might be generating that feeling. Let's say the thought is something like, "How dare she abandon me when I need her the most," and the accompanying feelings are of indignation and hurt. We can then ask ourselves what thought might be generating *those* feelings—in other words, "what am I telling myself about what's happening?"

Perhaps we will encounter a thought like, "I don't matter to her," and come across the accompanying feelings of insignificance. If we look beneath *these* feelings, we may then discover the thought that "I am insignificant" and the accompanying feelings of inadequacy. If we further unravel these feelings of inadequacy, tracing them all the way down to their underlying thought, we may arrive at a statement like, "I don't matter to me" and feel the associated feelings of hopelessness. As Forrest notes, when we arrive at this kind of self-defeating statement about who we are and what is our place in the world, we know that we have landed on our core belief. This is the knot at the center of our conflict, the central refrain around which our limbic harmony revolves.[32]

RIGHT WITHOUT WRONG,
ORDER WITHOUT DISORDER

There are many ways of untying such knots. One simple method, adapted from Byron Katie's *The Work,* is to invert the core belief into its opposite statement. "When we turn a troubling belief around and find examples of how its opposite is true," writes Forrest, "we often discern less painful ways of interpreting life."[33] In this case, we could invert the belief "I don't matter to me" into its opposite, "I *do* matter to me." We could then inventory specific ways we have cared for and prioritized ourselves. More important, we can begin to act *as if the inverted belief were true*—which amounts to acting from a different script.

As we come into contact with, and then begin to unravel, these formative knots in our psyche, we liberate ourselves into the possibility of genuine connection with others, as free and conscious players, unencumbered by projections. Instead of looking at others, we can see them; instead of controlling others, we can touch and move them, meeting at the level of the soul. For "when I am touched," writes Carse, "I am touched only as the person I am behind all the theatrical masks, but at the same time I am changed from within—and whoever touches me is touched as well." To enter into unscripted reality, then, is to enter into real intimacy with others such that both players are liberated from their stereotyped responses in the moment. "We do not touch by design," writes Carse. "Indeed, all designs are shattered by touching."[34]

To shatter a design is to see beyond a role-bound value judgment. It is to cherish the inherent worth of the individual, and to treasure the uniqueness of the limbic dance she offers, rather than evaluating her for her usefulness in leading us toward one or another finite goal. By setting down our filters—such as positive and negative, useful and inhibitive—we recover our awareness of the majesty of others, a majesty that, in its full expression, transcends all categories and extends into the infinite.

From here we apprehend, along with the Taoist sage Chuang-Tzu, that "he who wants to have right without wrong, order without disorder, does not understand the principles of heaven and earth. He does not know how things hang together."[35] For it is only by entering into the emotional worlds of others that we can experience something beyond the horizons of our known reality.

By surrendering to the dance between our world and this other world, we can give birth to a universe of shared possibilities. The novelist Vladimir Nabokov speaks to this when he says, "The work of art is invariably the creation of a new world, so that the first thing we should do is to study this new world as closely as possible, approaching it as something brand new, having no obvious connections with the world we already know."[36]

Working along similar lines, the authors of *A General Theory of Love* tell us that such an artist "loosens his grip on his own world and drifts, eyes open, into whatever relationship the [other] has in mind—even a connection so dark that it touches the worst in him."[37] In this "duet between minds, each has its own harmonies and the tendency to draw others into a compatible key," and each "finds parts of himself stirring in response to the particular magnetism of the emotional mind across from him."[38]

Because we no longer play the victim to our circumstances, we can harmonize with even the darkest of these melodies, meeting them with wonder and curiosity. Rather than being dragged into the darkness kicking and screaming, we can surrender and open to the descent—with its promise of disclosing something startling about the universe. We may then find, along with Jessica Benjamin, that "once such a . . . system gets going, it seems to move naturally in the direction of orienting to a deeper law of reality."[39]

Consider the case of Rick Doblin, founder of the Multidisciplinary Association for Psychedelic Studies. The son of conservative Jewish immigrants who came to America before the outbreak of World War II, Doblin "grew up thinking the whole world was Jewish. That was my education. All my parents' friends were Jewish. The neighbors were all Jewish. We went to temple. You're a little kid, you think your whole world is the universe."[40]

In his early twenties, Doblin had a profound dream that overlapped seamlessly with this cultural identity. The dream took him back to the Holocaust, where he witnessed "thousands of Jews lined up along a mass grave as the gunners open fire, toppling the bodies into the earth." He then sees that one man has managed to escape this fate by hiding underground for three days, "before emerging and fleeing to the woods, where he survives the war in hiding. The man then tells Doblin that he survived this horror only to deliver a message that Doblin should devote his life to promoting psychedelics as a cure for human ills and an insurance policy against another Holocaust. Then he expires."[41]

Doblin took this message in earnest and began fighting for the medicalization and legalization of psychedelics, just as the dream figure had asked him to. Central to Doblin's mission was his deep commitment to ensuring that his descendants would not have to suffer as his ancestors had. "I've always felt that the response to the Holocaust is helping people realize our common humanity," Doblin said. "And that there are many ways to do that, and psychedelic mystical experiences are one of the ways. And so I felt like what I'm doing is trying to prevent another Holocaust, and that's the deepest motivation."[42]

But two of Doblin's psychedelic-assisted explorations of our common humanity took him to some disturbingly dark corners of his psyche, revealing startling facts about himself, which called the finite boundaries of his identity into question. Doblin writes about the first of these sessions, in which he took the psychedelic compound DMT:

Had this insight that in the deepest recesses of who I think I am, this inner voice that's kind of always talking to you, that I was using English. And I didn't invent English. . . . It's all the product of all these people that came before me. So even in my most inner, private self, I'm intermixed with everything and everything's part of me. And it was all this beautiful stuff. And then I realized. . . . Well, if everything is part of you and you are part of everything, then Hitler is part of you too. It's inner. And that was very shattering for me . . . that if we want to claim that we're connected with everything, then it's not just the evil out there, that it's potentially in me.[43]

His language is telling. For to call the experience "shattering" is to acknowledge that his identification with the demonized other shattered the culture-bound identity that he had come to see as essential to his being. To shatter this identity is to recognize the true, interwoven nature of reality, in which there is no self or other, no Jew or Nazi, no clear line between right and wrong or good and evil.

This recognition deepened the next day, when he tried the drug ketamine. During the trip, Doblin saw himself "hovering behind Hitler as he's giving one of these speeches, like the Nuremburg rally kind of things. And the ketamine gave me a bit of remove so I didn't freak out—I was there but not there, so I didn't feel vulnerable in that way. And I saw him doing this speech, and I'm thinking, how do I get into his head, how do I help him not want to murder and kill, what can undo this evil? And then I saw the *heil Hitler* salute near the end of his speech. . . . He would . . . put up his hand, like that, and then everybody in the crowd would do it back to him. And I felt like it was the one pushing out this energy and the many pushing it back to him. And they would go back and forth. And the intensity was kind of increasing. And at that point I was just realizing there's no way to get into his head. It has to be voluntary. And he was getting so much from it. . . .[44]

"I felt this panic rising above me. And I felt that if I were to panic I would never be able to be effective in this world. I would just kind of turn away from that [darkness]. And then with ketamine you can still breathe. So I realized that if I just breathe it could help me with this fear. And then ironically came this idea that, rather than trying to change the mind of the one, we need to change the mind of the many. . . . They don't get as much out of it as Hitler did. . . . They're giving their power away to him. And that's where we need mass mental health."[45]

In other words, by identifying with the greatest evil, by getting into the mind of Hitler himself, Doblin clarified the direction he could take to prevent another genocide.

Gabor Maté, himself a survivor of the Holocaust, provides another telling illustration of the power of compassionately identifying with a demonized other. In *The Myth of Normal,* he and his son Daniel tell the story of Sue Hanish, an English woman who had her right leg blown off and her left foot severely damaged by an Irish Republican Army bomb that went off at London's Victoria Station.[46]

"Ever the adventurous sort," they write, "some years after the explosion she found herself in South Africa's KwaZulu-Natal wilderness on a peacemaking mission with, among others, several participants from Northern Ireland, veterans of the very organization whose bomb had mangled her body and altered her life forever. 'The idea,' she said, 'was to hear the other side of the story, to see each other's struggles, and to put us in an environment where we would need to protect one another.'[47]

"At some point the expedition had to ford a river. Sue's dilemma was that she could not expose her metallic prosthesis to water, and the anticipation made her quite agitated. She needn't have worried: plans had already been made for her safe and dry passage. Two men carried her across on their shoulders, one of them an IRA militant. 'The fact that it was an IRA guy, it made me absolutely overcome with emotion. I was crying and so was Don, the IRA man. The experience of working with these fellows made me realize just how damaged they had been by what had gone on in their lives before. Don himself was the youngest of seventeen. He had his first gun when he was eight, and he grew up in a children's home. He'd been in jail, he'd been bullied, and he'd been having a really tough time himself. He was carrying the burden of having killed people and not having a clear conscience. It was good for me to be with these people whose lives I had had no insight into before. I realized I could have easily been Don, had I grown up in those circumstances."[48]

Doblin and Sue's stories illustrate a key principle: When we make unscripted contact with others, we are inevitably drawn into a deeper order, into the underlying rhythm through which life dances itself into existence. We become more complex as players when we render ourselves fluid enough to surrender to the flux of this reality. Like Magister Ludi of Hesse's *The Glass Bead Game*, we may then in time become "so constituted that we can at any time be placed in a different position without offering resistance or losing our heads," however challenging those positions might be. For we can see, in every position of the game, an opportunity to awaken to another facet of our divinity, to remember that hidden secret: That we are God, and this is play.[49]

THE INFINITE GAME

This orientation toward unscripted play opens us up to what Carse calls the *infinite game*. Whereas the player of a finite game plays to win, the player of an infinite game plays to keep the game going.[50] There are therefore no spatial, temporal, or numerical limits to infinite play, as these limits would hinder the continuation of the game. "No world is marked with . . . barriers," writes Carse, "and there is no question of eligibility since anyone who wishes to play may play an infinite game."[51]

As infinite players, we seek to expose the voluntary nature of these barriers. For the interrelatedness of life, the fact that "whatever affects one directly affects all indirectly," reveals to us the arbitrariness of such limits and the absurdity of the separation they imply. We therefore play with the limitations and boundaries of others, not to cause harm, but to elicit an original, unscripted response—and to reveal the permeability of those limits in the process. We recognize that "to speak, or act, or think originally is to erase the boundaries of the self. It is to leave the territorial personality." And we orient every move toward this erasure, through which the personality is eschewed and the genius unfettered.

As we move from the linearity of theater into the open-endedness of poetry, we cultivate the vision to see life's obstacles as opportunities. This isn't to say that these obstacles can't be challenging; for the absence of such challenges would dissipate the potency of our game. The difference is that, whereas a finite player might resign himself to victimhood in the face of these challenges, an infinite player will expose them for what they truly are: openings into the depths of life. Moving through the painful constriction of these openings, she allows her creative genius to lead the game to somewhere new.

For example, Gabor and Daniel Maté tell us of a woman named Julia, who learned to repress "her feelings to protect everyone else's"—a pattern that eventually contributed to her developing arthritis. "In contravention of all cultural mores," they write, "Julia expressed gratitude for her rheumatoid arthritis. 'It saved me,' she said. 'It was my body's way of saying, 'wake up, wake up, you're not helping yourself holding this much anger and rage deep down inside.' Anger and rage are not feelings I want to hold on to, but I do see them as guides that let me know that something in my life is out of balance. I get [rheumatoid] flare-ups maybe once a year now. When one shows up, I just accept that it's here and there is something I can do about it, something more to learn from it. . . . I have beautiful conversations with my rheumatoid arthritis these days—it makes me want to cry."[52]

To be clear, this does not mean that the infinite player, by way of her resourcefulness, "wins" by successfully eradicating such symptoms, even in cases where those symptoms might lead to death. For to play against death is to press for an outcome—the preservation of the finite body—and to press for such an outcome is to forfeit the incomparable richness of open-ended play. From a place of deep surrender, the infinite player delivers her body over to her experiences, taking even death into the boundaries of her game, so that she can discover who she is under all conditions. "Since the boundaries of death are always part of the play," writes Carse, "the infinite player does not die at the end of play, but in the course of play."[53]

As infinite players, we know that our inward divinity did not descend into this world merely to cling to its forms. We know the hidden unity with which heaven and earth hang together. We know the infinite game will continue in others, and that in any moment the highest play is to surrender. Like Magister Ludi, the game master, our lives then become "a perpetual transcending, a progression from stage to stage—as music moves from theme to theme, from tempo to tempo, playing each out to the end, completing each and leaving it behind, never tiring, never sleeping, forever wakeful, forever in the present."[54]

6

On Ritual and Union

We must go down to the very foundations of life. For any merely superficial ordering of life that leaves its deepest needs unsatisfied is as ineffectual as if no attempt at order had ever been made.[1]

—I CHING

Between the poles of the conscious and the unconscious . . . hang the body and the mind . . . between the arms of the beloved, in the ecstasy of love's joy.[2]

—KABIR

THE VERY FOUNDATIONS

As we progressively unravel the knots of our conditioning, we may find ourselves venturing down into what the I Ching calls *the very foundations of life*. In this strange and wondrous primordial terrain, we encounter the energies of sex and aggression, rage and power, and everything else we had suppressed and rejected in service to the maintenance of our finite personality. The totality of these energies, which the psychologist Rollo May terms the *daemonic*, arise "from the ground of being rather than the self as such." Their sources lie "in those realms where the self is rooted in natural forces which go beyond the self and are felt as the grasp of fate upon us."[3]

Moving beyond the conditioned, disparate criteria of right and wrong, we enter an intimate relationship with the rejected elements of our being. To surrender to this urge for intimacy is to surrender to the power of Eros, the beating heart at the very foundation of life. Eros is the magnet that would draw the scattered fragments of the psyche into a unified self while simultaneously celebrating and fortifying their polarity. In wedding the finite to the infinite, Eros exposes both the tremulousness of the naked heart and the immutability of the inward spirit—drawing the two into a mysterious, dynamic unity that orients its polarity toward a higher order of reality. Eros knows when to gently nudge us out of our habituated grooves and when to shock us out of our conditioned reality, when to trace its fingertips across our boundaries and, in doing so, define us; when to seize us from the elemental depths and set us all ablaze with the fire of our divinity. Eros brings together not only love but also hate, not only softness but also aggression, guiding us into the ground of our being, while simultaneously extending us into unfettered contact with our environment.

Saint Augustine rightly defined Eros as "the power which drives men toward God."[4] What he failed to mention is that it does so first and foremost by driving us into everything that we would consider to be the opposite of God—into our lust and our vitriol, our envy and our resentment, our bitterness and our fear. Eros magnetizes the neglected, suppressed, rejected, and disowned aspects of our being, bringing them to the surface of our awareness and insisting that we meet them with love and devotion: that we put down our weapons and surrender to the genuine relief of having remembered the divinity in the darkness.

In other words, Eros draws us toward the other in a manner that reflects the other's presence within our very soul. We are then just as likely to recognize the other as an externalized reflection of our inner landscape as we are to recognize our inner landscape as the true home of the externalized other. Eros seduces us into playing with these distinctions, with the boundaries between self and other, inside and outside, drawing us into that boundless expanse of unprecedented uncertainty, where we experience the other in ourselves and the other-than-ourselves experiences us. It "does not guide just one or another part of our being," writes the Syrian mystic Iamblichus, "but all of them at once, and it extends to us the whole administration of us, even as it has been allotted to us from all the regions of the universe."[5]

This is why the Lila myth elevates the Erotic—with its rapturous culmination in Krishna's love-play with his maidens, in that moonlit field where he "embraced them in nine ways, kissed them in eight ways, and cohabited with them in sixteen ways."[6] Krishna's Lila shows us that to be a playful god is to be an Erotic god; the two are inseparable. Both play and Eros evoke an attitude of unconditional surrender, a willingness to say yes in every moment, to increase our attention and refine our engagement until even the most challenging conflicts are transfigured into beauty, rapture, laughter, and joy. Both play and Eros stretch the boundaries of self and world to include everything: the darkness and the light, the inner and the outer, the conventional and the prohibited, the obsessive and the serene.

A playful universe, then, is an Erotic universe, in which all things outstretch themselves vulnerably toward one another from their polar opposition, yearning for the intimacy of contact, the ecstasy of release, and the continuation of their play. In the love-drunk playground of Krishna's field, all players delightfully unveil themselves, unabashedly removing all impediments to intimacy. In the otherworld of this Erotic dance, there is no forbidden zone or restricted portion of either body or soul. No part of the self is off limits, no desire or hunger is too taboo. Here, in liberating themselves from all proscribed modes of engagement, the maidens discover how their bodies want to touch and move—how the organic fluidity of the body would express itself if left to its own desires, unencumbered by the confining clichés of sexual norms.

ON RITUAL INTIMACY

Erotic play reaches its highest form in the act of ritual. Formally, rituals and games have all the same elements: There is a boundary, or magic circle; a goal, which could be anything; a feedback system, which communicates how successfully our play is moving us toward that goal; and voluntary participation. By coalescing these elements, a ritual, like a game, creates a laboratory for consciousness, an arena for visceral power to unleash, and archetypal dynamics to engage in free play.

The distinction between a ritual and a game can be hard to discern at times, particularly when we consider formal games from their inner dimension, or when we consider rituals whose outer structures match perfectly with those of a formal game—such as the ritual ball game found throughout ancient Mesoamerica, which we will later explore. The key distinction is that, in a ritual, the inner and outer dimensions are seamless, in the sense that their goals are the same: The union with the transcendent other and the resultant transformation of consciousness.

In other words, while we may either emphasize or disregard the inner dimension of play during a game, shutting the outside world from the designated field of play, we may not do so during a ritual— even one that looks and feels identical to a game. For to disregard the interior aspect of a ritual is to fall out of the invisible, sacred order that it has so deliberately conjured into visible form and return to a finite time and space in which no genuine transformation can occur.

Through the magic of ritual, we can enter into intimate contact with a dismembered aspect of our being and re-member or rejoin it to our self-image, expanding the boundaries of our identity in the process. In other words, ritual allows for a deepening of our capacity to know and express our essential nature, as well as a widening of the limits on who and what we are willing to consider to be a part of that nature. We reunite ourselves with the environment from which our scriptedness had estranged us, and reconcile the interior aspects of ourselves that we had cast as the antagonists in our theatrical conflicts.

A ritual, like a game, is fundamentally a sensory and sensuous experience. The gentle burn of sandalwood caresses our skin and soothes our nervous system; the physical gesture of breathing its smoke informs our consciousness that we have integrated, and will continue to integrate, the other into our being; the rhythmic pulse of the drumbeat and the harmonic reverberations of the ritual song awaken our bones to the musicality of the cosmos and the poetry of our place within it; the coordinated movement of bodies in motion entrains our limbic systems to the emergent symphony of the group and its genius, carrying us upward or perhaps downward into the mystery.

Dr. Andrew Newberg, a neuroscientist whose work focuses on the intersection of biological processes and mystical states, speaks to this sensory element when he writes that "ritual dancing, singing, or chanting can drive the brain's frontal cortex into producing ineffable, pleasurable feelings. In combination with other activities often part of a ritual—fasting, repetition or call and response, hyperventilation or inhalation of incense—this multisensory stimulation can affect the body in ways that lead to altered states."[7]

THE ROOTS OF CREATION

In his book *Neurotheology,* Newberg suggests that human rituals may have emerged from animal courtship behavior, which underwent increasing elaboration and differentiation during the evolutionary course of neurological development.

These rituals created a natural point of departure toward mystical states of union, "since the primary goal of the mating ritual is to lose yourself and become one with another."[8]

By activating their primal need for reproduction, by harnessing and channeling the biological imperatives that lie at the foundations of their beings, the male and female birds ascend to heights of ecstasy inaccessible even by flight. By losing themselves in each other, the two rediscover that original oneness from which the kaleidoscopic forms arise.

An ancient Chinese proverb conveys a similar insight when it refers to "sexual intercourse [as] the human counterpart of the cosmic process."[9] For the cosmic process sways back and forth between unity and duality; between dissolution into the ground of being and differentiation into the world of appearances; between compulsivity and freedom; between form and formlessness. In the alternating rhythm of this Erotic play, the tension of separation builds only to resolve itself at a higher unity. Here, our biological programming draws us paradoxically into an un-programmatic terrain, into a world defined by spontaneous freedom and tender vulnerability.

CONJURING THE PLAYGROUND

The spatial and temporal boundaries imposed by the ritual container create a world apart, a magical dimension in which rules, values, and qualities differ drastically from those of the mundane world beyond its perimeter. As Huizinga points out, "formally speaking, there is no distinction whatever between marking out a space for a sacred purpose and marking it out for purposes of sheer play."[10] The difference has less to do with formality and more to do with intentionality, or metacommunication: while the boundaries of a game communicate that "this is play," the boundaries of a ritual communicate that "this play is sacred."

The potency of this sacred play is a function of the containment provided by the magic circle. For "if the boundaries of a sacred space are too permeable," writes the religious scholar and Jungian analyst Robert

Moore, "it does not get hot enough for a transformation to occur." The ritual boundaries contain the fire of transformation, "keeping the vessel hot" enough to melt the formative knots from which our scripts arise.[11] By disorienting us from the mundane world in which these scripts are nested, sacred space allows us to reorient ourselves to the true nature of reality, as well as the originality of our expression within it. The intoxication of our ritual play, then, paradoxically becomes a pathway to our sobriety from the narcotic slumber of our social conditioning.

The image of Krishna and his flute song conveys the forcefulness of this rapturous tear from the mundane. For the play-god's call to ritual "pulls virtuous women from their homes and drags them by their hair" into another world.[12] The intoxicating call of the hierophany, the blazing manifestation of the sacred amid the felt tediousness of the surrounding order, so enchants the maidens that their garments slip to the ground, exposing their true nature. The veils of socialization and its scripts fall away as the electric pulse of the living god illuminates a hidden dimension of reality whose rules break not only social but even natural law. For in this place, "chaste ladies forget their lords, wise men forget their wisdom, and clinging vines shake loose from their trees."

In forgetting these social scripts, we remember the unscripted spontaneity of nature. We make intimate contact with the beauty of life, which we experience as an irresistible lover, as handsome as Krishna, as haunting as his song, as arousing as his touch and alluring as his playful glances. All stereotyped behaviors fall away as the rapture of Eros sets our hearts ablaze and lights up our limbs with its sacred fire. Thrown into this other world, whose rhythm carries us into higher octaves of love, we remember the suppleness with which the body was always meant to move. And as we sway along in concert with its harmony, our senses awaken to the invisible threads that unite child's play with primal power, poetic insight with mystic intuition, mantic vision with oracular speech.

ACTUALIZATION BY REPRESENTATION

Of course, the drawing of a boundary alone cannot trigger such an experience. The archetypal powers from which the ritual ecstasy arise must also be invoked. Though there are many ways to call these powers into a ritual space, most of them are variations on what Huizinga calls *actualization by representation.* By assigning specific symbolic value to a person, object, or natural feature within the magic circle, we can exteriorize an interior process, lending it sensuous form and opening it up to the play of our Erotic intelligence. Huizinga characteristically likens this process to the make-believe of a child, who imagines, and then enters into, another reality through the course of his play: "something different, something more beautiful, or more sublime, or more dangerous than what usually is." In this imaginal playground, we direct our consciousness toward the representation of a "cosmic event," allowing us to "participate in the sacred happening itself."[13]

In ritual, we stimulate the symbolic power of our consciousness and channel it toward our goal: of re-enchanting our image of the world; of reinterpreting every facet of self and other in light of the interwoven unity of being. The deliberate projection of our unconscious contents in embodied form moves us toward this goal by affording us an opportunity to grapple with our own darkness—to reconcile the repressed and rejected aspects of ourselves, and in doing so, direct their energy toward the cultivation of a more complex and integrated self. This integrative power is implicit in the etymology for the word *symbolic,* which derives from the Greek *sym-bollein,* meaning "to throw together" or "to unite."[14]

DUALITY AND UNION

Let's consider the Mesoamerican ball-game ritual in light of these distinctions. Although we know little about the rules of the game or how it was played, the scarcity of our technical knowledge is compensated by the richness of what we know about its symbolic meaning.

Every aspect of the game was directed toward a union of opposites, which the players actualized at multiple, simultaneous levels throughout the course of their play. At one level, the two opposing teams represented this opposition, which was contained within the unity of the single ballcourt. At another level, the ballcourt itself represented a duality, as it was split into two discrete and uncrossable sides, each of which was considered "to be on the other shore of a river."[15] Yet the court's duality, too, was contained within the larger unity of the single game, which embraced both the opposing teams and their respective sides of the playground.

From here, the thematic layers of duality and union become increasingly multifaceted. For every time a player struck the ball to the other side of the ballcourt—sending it flying across that cosmic river—he both accentuated his opposition and enacted his longing for contact. And because the court, in its sunkenness, represented the underworld, as the ball soared from one side of the court to the other, rising and falling with the natural arc of gravity, it enacted in microcosm the celestial rhythm of the sun, rising into the heavens each day and descending each night into the world below.[16] This motif was further amplified by the mythic literature, in which the game was culturally situated, and the court engravings, in which the game was physically situated: contemporary texts contained illustrations of a "ballgame played between the Lords of the Day and the Lords of the Night,"[17] and some ballgame reliefs displayed images of the "descending sun god."[18]

By way of their symbolic descent into that primordial underworld, and their pledge to play with the inherent volatility of its terrain, the players volunteered to struggle with and reconcile the opposites within their very being, discovering felt solutions to apparent contradictions. If successful, these solutions would nourish their communities, both figuratively and literally: for to play with the cosmic cycles of darkness and light was to play with the seasonal rhythms of agricultural fertility that coincided with those cycles. By actualizing the movements of the sun, moon, and other celestial bodies through the symbolism of the game, the players directed the heavens toward the continuity and flourishing of life.[19] This is why ballcourt reliefs typically included carvings of "flowering and fruiting plants,"[20] and why the game has been referred to as "the cycle of the pivot of creation."[21]

In *The Sport of Life and Death*, the Mexican historian María Teresa Uriarte further unravels the symbolic meaning of these carved reliefs. Focusing on a selection of representations that "at first glance may seem unconnected," such as "snakes, crocodiles, toads, turtles . . . butterflies [and] jaguars," she argues that every symbol in the game amplifies the same underlying theme of unity in duality, as well as the associated theme of liminality.[22] The two are in fact inseparable, as liminality is the transitional state through which union is made possible. The butterfly transforms from one state to another, and so symbolizes the state of being in-between, as well as the transformation that results from such a state.[23] The snake is eternally shedding its skin and so enacting the cycles of death and rebirth, while containing both within its transitional body. The jaguar, as a land predator that can swim and hunt in water, expresses the capacity to move between worlds—to literally cross to the other shore of a river.[24] And the crocodile, turtle, and toad also move freely between the solidity of the surface world and the fluidity of the water world.[25] By representing this symbolism in the carved ambiance of their playground, the players actualized their own potential to move in and out of multiple worlds, of alternate dimensions of perception and experience.

This liminality was further amplified by the symbol system the players encoded into the human body itself. For the human body is also two-in-one, in that it has a lower half, an upper half, and a liminal midpoint between the two. The anthropologist Susan Gillespie highlights this division by pointing to the illustrations on one of the game's implements, called a *palma*, which depicts only the lower body on one side and the upper body on the other. This liminality is accentuated by the fact that most ballgame rituals only allowed their players to strike the ball with the midpoint of the body, typically around the hips. "This means the ball could touch a player only at the boundary between the upper and lower body," she writes, "further reiterating the conceptual division of the body noted above for the . . . palma, an object which was worn at the player's waist, at the conceptual boundary."[26]

In other words, the ballgame player contained both the celestial and the chthonic worlds within the dynamic potency of his ritual body. By exteriorizing his inner landscape, by projecting out the depths of his psyche and lending his inner images sensuous form, he could then re-assimilate these contents from a higher vantage point, from which the polarity of opposition could be unified into a singular field of vision. In the ritual apotheosis, the inward divinity of the player would take possession, charging his movements with rhythm, beauty, and power, such that this expanded consciousness could persist long after the ritual had ended. The conflicting aspects of the psyche, symbolized by the oppositional strife of the competing teams, could come together in an erotic embrace, a mystical marriage through which a new self would be born.

ALCHEMIZING THE OTHER

The same mechanism applies whether the symbols we embody are cosmic or more personal in nature. In either case, the liminality of the ritual space allows us to adopt a transitional identity fluid enough for us to freely slip in and out of various roles—including those roles that differ radically from our scripted personae. Through the embodied imagination of our ritual play, we can dramatically inhabit the energy of our enemies and, seeing life through their eyes, integrate their perspective into our consciousness. We can come to know, in a viscerally personal way, what it feels like to be the antagonists in our dramas. And we can do so from the inside out, not as a *them* but as a *me,* as an experiencing subject with his own thoughts, feelings, and sensations. In doing so, we can restore the dehumanized other to its humanity. For "the spontaneous impulse of the spirit to identify itself with something other than itself for the sheer delight of play," writes Joseph Campbell, "transubstantiates the world—in which, actually, all things are not quite as real, permanent, terrible, important, or logical as they seem."[27]

In *Love and Will*, Rollo May describes an indigenous West African ritual directed toward this transubstantiation. He tells us that whenever a villager in the Yoruba community is in a state of crisis, he first consults a shaman to assess the inner roots of his conflict. The whole village then comes together to perform a ritual dance in service to the resolution of this person's crisis.[28] By situating this ritual transformation within a communal dance, the player is free to renegotiate his relationships with his larger community: The dance itself both melts down the rigidity of scripted relationships and actualizes, by representation, an embodied remembrance of the larger, cosmic dance in which those relationships are ultimately situated. The anthropologist Victor Turner refers to the resultant state of consciousness as *communitas,* which he defines as "a direct, immediate, and total confrontation of human identities, . . . [in which] we feel that it is important to relate directly to another person as he presents himself in the here and now . . . free from all culturally defined encumbrances of his role."[29]

While the encircling community sways in remembrance of life's rhythms, the suffering individual takes center stage and identifies with the imagined adversary of his dramatic conflict. May describes one case in which a villager who had been struggling with impotence dressed up in his mother's clothing and danced around like her for a length of time. "This reveals to us" the shaman's recognition that "such a man's impotence is connected with his relationship with his mother—ostensibly an over-dependence on her which he, in his own self-system, has denied. What is necessary for the 'cure,' thus, is that he confronts and comes to terms with this . . . in himself."[30] In other words, by setting himself aside and playing the part of an overbearing mother, he can reconcile the tension between his conscious personality and his internalized negative mother image, freeing the energy that had been tied up in that primal conflict and, in doing so, liberating himself to redirect it toward a healthy sexuality.

ON POWER AND OTHER TABOOS

The ritual space allows us to safely and voluntarily descend into these haunting dimensions of the psyche, the realms in which our shadows lie. We commit to loving the whole of existence by taking even the most vilified substances into ourselves and expanding our self-conception to contain and include that material. And we do so in a spirit of play, with the levity that would allow us to move lightly in and out of even the heaviest terrain.

The *pancatattva* ritual practiced by left-handed tantrics in India encapsulates this orientation. During the ritual, the devotee plays with the conventional boundaries of his society by partaking "of things that are considered particularly vile or unclean, such as meat, wine, and sexual intercourse (the five forbidden things, the *pancatattva*)."[31] Here, the demonized substance is taken quite literally into the self in order to integrate the shadow of the culture's prohibitions. "In this way," writes Indologist Heinrich Zimmer, the devotee "breaks within himself the tension of the 'forbidden' and resolves everything in light. . . . Therewith comes release from the world-illusion . . . release through its full enjoyment or realization."[32]

By playing with the boundaries of convention, tantric practitioners are free to dissolve the arbitrary divisions in their psyche and, in doing so, bring an end to their compartmentalization. With each reintegration, with every open-armed embrace of the forbidden or the shamed, they land deeper into unity with the divinity of this world.

This intersection of playing with taboo and playing with identity lies at the heart of BDSM, a form of erotic play that combines elements of theater, games, and rituals all in one art form. The term is an acronym, referring to a broad spectrum of activities that involve some element of bondage and discipline (B/D), dominance and submission (D/s), and sadism and masochism (S/M) in an atmosphere of trust, safety, and consent. By consciously and overtly designing and enacting these scenes with trusted playmates, we may safely explore the darker corners of the "do-er and done-to relationship" described by Benjamin in chapter 5. Here we bring the covert games to light, consciously and wholeheartedly consenting to an experience that may even purposefully emulate a scenario that lies outside our range of play. The option is present in both as a shift in perception, not as a means to trivialize our experience but to acknowledge our own divine potential, to be liberated into autotelos—playing to play. From that perspective, the challenges we are confronted with appear as the loving opponent, asking us "Even here? Even here?" and drawing us further out into the field of play.

The diversity of activities that fall under the umbrella of BDSM make it hard to define the term precisely, but most definitions center around the free exchange of power in the context of play. Some are physical, some are verbal, some exist in a variety of planes or are very explicitly limited, but they are performed to deliver their players an experience, from the vulnerability of stepping into an unfamiliar role to the power of reclaiming desire and play in a position we had so often before misplaced them. "The key to understanding BDSM," writes professional dominatrix Cléo DuBois, "is that it is a negotiated exchange between adults who trust each other."[33] Working along similar lines, the sexuality writers Dossie Easton and Janet Hardy describe BDSM as "power games for fun instead of profit."[34]

Anytime we play with power—manipulating it, wielding it, taking it, or giving it away—we are engaging in a radically taboo activity. No additional whips or handcuffs are required to render consensual power games an edgy form of play, as we live in a culture that either demonizes power or denies its existence. For many, power brings to mind the painful dramas of our past, in which we experienced it as something exerted upon us without our consent. When we think of power, we tend to think of persecution, bullying, ruthlessness, victimization, torment, intimidation, brutality, and abuse. To use Mary Parker Follet's term, we typically think of *power over*—power over someone we see as powerless, done-to, victimized, and abused. Someone helpless, weak, impotent, exploited, tortured, terrorized, or taken advantage of.

But neither the denial nor the pathologization of power can change the fact that, when we open our eyes to it, power is everywhere: between government and citizen, employer and employee, father and daughter, teacher and student, priest and parishioner, waiter and customer, prostitute and client, addict and drug. Rather than suppressing or ignoring these dynamics, BDSM allows for the conscious creation of elegant containers in which to consensually and safely explore what they feel like, in the context of connection and care. Unlike ordinary life, in which our experience of our own agency is clouded by the theatricality of our scripts, we can design scenes in which participants know they are playing voluntarily. As Easton and Hardy put it, we can "imitate the outward appearance of those grim real-world struggles for power, while building in the safeguards we need to keep us from being genuinely harmed."[35]

Our overt consent to, and participation in, the designing of these scenes allows us to make the movement from power-over to power-with. We discover that all true power is shared power, and that shared power elevates the status of every player in the game. BDSM players can freely share their power in this way because their play occurs in an atmosphere of trust and safety. "The element of trust is very important," writes DuBois, "as are the elements of negotiation and informed consent and revealing your desire. That means talking ahead of time about what you *do* want, what you *might* want, and what you *don't* want to do, and agreeing on 'safe words' to say out loud, to slow or stop the action."[36] Each aspect of a container can be designed in advance, providing a structure to navigate the liminal terrain between the known and unknown portions of our psyche. We need only ever play with edges we feel we can trust our partner and ourselves to consciously stay in.

The feedback system allows us to further relax our vigilance by bringing us back into connection during moments of high sensation. These communications can be as simple as the safe words of *green*, "keep going"; *yellow*, "slow down"; and *red*, "stop now, I am out of my range." These safe words allow all players to drop into a scene and surrender to its dynamism while remaining confident that they won't harm or be harmed along the way. Safe words allow for an exploration of grayness— we can stay in that zone of pleasurable pain, of ecstatic agony, and discover what naturally emerges from within us in that place.

At subtler levels, the feedback system includes all the sensations, sounds, and intuitions that are shared between both players in a scene. For the heightened energy of a scene concentrates our senses and opens our nervous systems to read and respond to the nuanced interplay of energy dancing between us. We can feel for the subtlest shift in our partner's body—the slight fluttering of a heartbeat, the faint quickening of a breath—reading this living language and responding to the immediacy of its messages. Eventually, a resonance occurs, through which the hidden musicality of the scene begins to coordinate our movements, swaying us toward a more inclusive reality.

PLAYING WITH THE SHADOW

From the outside, it may look like a Dominant is doing something to her submissive by, for example, flogging him, in reality the submissive has not only volunteered to undergo such an experience, he has overtly asked for it. By eroticizing the taboo feelings of helplessness, humiliation, and weakness, the submissive can convert the shame that ordinarily accompanies him into orgasmic pleasure—and he gets to be the center of attention in the process. In *Sexual Outsiders,* the kink-informed therapists David Ortmann and Richard Sprott go so far as to say that "the state of submission may be one of the most powerful states of BDSM consciousness for the very fact that the act of giving over one's power to a trusted Dominant is, in and of itself, an act of extreme power and one that should not be taken lightly."[37] And the Dominant is usually just as happy to receive this power as the submissive is to give it, for it provides her with an avenue to explore her own taboo feelings and behaviors, which would be inappropriate in another context. "It's immensely liberating," write Easton and Hardy, "for a top to find out that there's a place where the top's 'dark side'—cruelty, bossiness, bullying, or nastiness—is not only tolerated, but appreciated." [38]

What distinguishes the resulting dynamic in a do-er and done-to relationship is that both players in a D/s scene are playing toward the emergent third. They set their compass on unity and hold fast to the flexibility of mind that would allow for this living, breathing energy to build and circulate between them. In a sense, then, the term *Dominant* is a misnomer. For, although, on one level, the Dominant overtly consents to wield the power the submissive has given them, to drive all participants deeper into increasingly shadowy edges of their psyche, on another level, they are playing from a state of total and complete surrender: to the spirit of play, and the archetypal dynamics it draws out of them; to the daemonic power within, whose roots penetrate into our very foundations; to the Eros that would wed our survival instinct to our sexual impulse and channel them both in service to unity.

By allowing these darker dimensions of our being to rise up to the surface of our consciousness, to come out of the shadows and into the soft moonlight of Erotic play, we can liberate ourselves from the need to compulsively enact them through covert games. To move toward this liberation is to move toward the recognition of innate beauty in every position in the dramas of our lives, as well as our creative capacity to reappraise the meaning, if not reshape the form, of these dramas. The simple interplay of the Dominant and submissive archetypes, within the context of deliberate, consensual, and conscious play undertaken in an atmosphere of trust and safety, provides us with an elegant tool toward this end. We can consciously script a scene in which to re-create painful, and even formative dramas from our past—experiences where we felt unsafe and where our agency felt out of reach. As Easton writes, "We can script a scene so we get to be child, parent, brat, hero, betrayer, betrayed. . . . The possibilities are endless."[39] More important, we can rewrite the ending of these dramas, or reappraise our interpretation of the overall experience, by playing their dynamics out with a loving, caring, and attuned partner in the safety of a consciously choreographed scene. "As we eroticize these tales from our deepest mythology," write Easton and Hardy, "we inject our self-rejection with the healing energy of the life force, with Eros, and confirm our newly enlarged sense of self with the affirmation of orgasm."[40]

For example, if we had a history of abusive relationships, we might choose to embody one of our abusers in a scene. But, to do so, we would have to be willing to fully inhabit his energy, to allow our inner villain to move and direct us. For there is a distinction between playing a role and being played through by an archetype—our own projection of the role we perceived our abuser embodying. In the former case, we are merely saying the words and dressed in the costume associated with our preconceived stereotype; in the latter, we are emptying ourselves enough of our fixed role and identity to be overtaken by a distinct energy of that other lurking within us, with its own way of responding to a situation. Rather than trying to "act like," we slow down and allow it to spontaneously arise and move through us. We venture into an unknown country and allow ourselves to be astonished by the freshness of its terrain, as well as its genuine beauty. We assume the kind of unconditional reception that would allow this energy to inhabit us entirely, with no friction, with no inner discrimination against its qualities, no selective filtering of acceptability or unacceptability. We become everything we had previously hated, everything we had villainized, and retain the consciousness of mind to be present with what it feels like to embody that archetype in connection with another.

We may then discover that there is tremendous vulnerability in identifying with the archetypal villain—especially if that archetype diverges radically from our typical, everyday identity. Easton tells of a scene she played out years ago with her coauthor, which speaks to this vulnerability: "We had planned a script in which a prom queen (me) gets kidnapped and ravished by a juvenile delinquent (Janet). . . . Afterward, after the rewarding sex that brought us more or less back to ourselves . . . Janet, now naked, came up to me and asked, in a very small voice, if I could please cuddle her for a while. So we wrapped the erstwhile tough guy in my pink skirts and hugged and stroked till she felt safe again. . . . That was the first appearance of my coauthor's precious inner villain—we have played with him quite happily many times since."[41]

It is obvious that we would only ever play out our inner villain in partnership with a consenting submissive who would love nothing more than to be on the receiving end of its torture. In fully embodying the archetype, we take on their motivations, their cares, their self-concern. We discover empathy with the other and even value for this aspect of ourselves, aided by the reception of the submissive.

Easton illustrates the alchemical power of a submissive's arousal by describing another scene, which she used to transmute the pain of having been dumped by a lover: "I negotiated with a friend of mine to top her, and she offered to provide a screen on which I could project all these bad feelings. After all, they weren't about her, and she is a great lover of intensity. After I warmed her up, we dove deeply into caning—me caning her, carefully and ferociously. I felt my rage and self-loathing flowing from my heart down my arm through the cane into her. She was my crucible, together we were melting down this anguish and forging it into something new and bright. As we do in intense play, I would from time to time move up to her face to check in and make sure she was all right. Toward the end of this, when I checked in once again, she turned and looked up at me with a shining face and a huge grin and said, 'I'm great, I'm fabulous. I love your shadow.' And in that moment, I loved my shadow too."[42]

In a scene like this, the submissive becomes the catalyst of our transformation, illuminating the beauty of the archetype at play within us.

Through "the alchemy of 'as if,'"[43] our embodied integration of the villain within us naturally resolves the tension of otherness and, with it, the need to project that aspect onto those around us. We can recognize and reconcile the darkness in our own being. No longer will we need to run from its energy. No longer will we need to seek the covert payoff of feeling outraged by its reflection in the other. We can love this part of ourselves back to its original nature, seeing in it the devotional essence beneath the coarseness it had previously presented with—due in no small part to our unconscious suppression. We can recognize the beauty and the generosity that it brings, for how its polarizing energy can push us, and push our partners, into otherwise inaccessible edges of consciousness. And we can do so mindfully, within the safety of our boundaries.

This kind of play lends a redemptive quality to ritual: We can feel the tenderness in agony, the devotion in violence, the generosity in rage, and the intimacy in conflict. Confirming the psychologist Peter Levine's insight, we can find that "the conscious containment and reflection upon our wild and primal urges enlivens us. . . . Rather than automatically reacting to (or suppressing) our instincts, we can explore them mindfully, through the vehicle of sensate awareness." In the sacred space of our ritual playground, we can "unveil our instincts as they live within us, rather than being alienated from them or forcibly driven by them."[44]

INTO THE BASEMENT

In the loving arms of our ritual container, and in the presence of a caring and trustworthy partner, we may even choose to re-create specific, painful scenes from our past—experiences in which we felt victimized or terrorized. And we can do so from a place of conscious intentionality. By retaining the mindfulness to stay firmly tethered to the body, and the sensations that flood through it during the course of our play, we can allow ourselves to be enlivened by the sensory and emotional saturation of the scene. This mindfulness alone may be sufficient to elicit a powerful healing, liberating us from the tendency to identify with our painful memories. For "trauma," writes psychologist Gabor Maté, "does not reside in the external event that induces physical or emotional pain— nor even in the pain itself—but in our becoming stuck in our primitive responses to painful events. Trauma is caused when we are unable to release blocked energies, to fully move through the physical/emotional reactions to hurtful experiences. Trauma is not what happens to us, but what we hold inside in the absence of an empathetic witness."[45]

In *Sexual Outsiders*, David Ortmann tells the story of his patient who used a D/s scene to re-create and move through stuck energy from his traumatic childhood, in the presence of an empathetic witness. A confident and well-dressed corporate executive, Darren initially made no mention of his childhood trauma, or the BDSM play he hoped would allow him to heal from it. He shared only that he had been struggling with low self-esteem, mild depression, and a speech impediment that he felt had been interfering with his career, although Dr. Ortmann had never witnessed the impediment personally. For the first few months of their work together, Darren evaded nearly all of Dr. Ortmann's attempts to learn about his childhood. The most he was willing to share was that his father had abandoned him and his mother when he was eleven; that she had raised him on her own until he'd left for college; and that she had died when he was twenty—a fact he reported with no emotion.[46]

That all changed three and a half months into their work together when, with no advance notice, Darren's wife, Alicia, accompanied him to one of his sessions. Without any prompting, the two of them spent much of that first session divulging, with great pleasure and specificity, every detail of their sex lives—which involved extensive BDSM play and was extremely satisfying for them both. The only area they reported any issue with was impact play on Darren's bottom. "It was physically and psychologically unbearable," a fact that Alicia had discovered by accident early in their relationship, when she'd spanked him during a night of especially hot sex.[47] "'I freaked out!' Darren said. 'After the third or fourth smack, I went blank, broke down, lost my erection, and cried. I went fetal. It was unexpected and humiliating. . . . Having my bottom hit released something in me and once it was released there was no turning back. Alicia and I talked all night.'"[48]

When Dr. Ortmann asked what they talked about, Darren told him: "M-m-my m-m-mother."[49]

The two of them then proceeded to describe Darren's traumatic childhood, which they both suspected had triggered his stuttering and which Darren had come to therapy to address. They told him that Darren's father had left when he was seven, not eleven, and had done so without saying goodbye. They told him that Darren's mother had spent the next several years in an uncomfortably affectionate relationship with him, and though there had been no sexual abuse, it was clear that she had been using him to fill the emptiness her husband had left behind. "They went on 'dates' to the movies and were always 'a couple' at family events like weddings and holiday gatherings." And they told him that Darren's relationship with his mother had taken a sudden and dramatic turn when he turned twelve years old. "She'd say things like: I was turning out just like my father; she'd yell at me for stupid things, and then not talk to me for hours."[50]

One day, after Darren spilled iced tea on a tablecloth, the relationship turned violent. She slapped him in the face, sent him to his room, and, upon meeting him there, demanded that he take off his clothes and lay on the bed. She then proceeded to spank him "really hard with a wooden-back brush. It was the first time he'd been struck by either parent, so it came out of nowhere for him." Adding insult to injury, she insisted that he not cry or make any sound during the beatings. "She said she would teach him to be quiet. That was the first of many beatings, punishments that took on an almost ritual-like quality and increased in frequency and ferocity over time. Those first beatings also coincided with . . . the time his stammer began."[51] When Dr. Ortmann asked Darren how he thought these beatings might have brought about his stuttering, he said that his mother had required Darren to stay totally silent during the beatings: "I never made a sound. After that first beating in the bedroom with the brush and the second one in the basement, no matter how hard she hit me, I never cried. I never made a sound. I lost my voice in that basement."[52]

Darren and Alicia then told Dr. Ortmann why they had come to him in the first place: They were planning to design a scene in which Darren could replay the experience of those beatings, with Alicia stepping in as the abusive mother; only this time he would be able to yell, scream, curse, and cry to his heart's content. Within the safety of their container, and in the presence of his loving and empathetic partner, he would scream and cry and unleash the years of repressed rage and betrayal he had kept inside since adolescence.[53] "The goal was catharsis through vocalization and a reclamation of power by his consenting to the same physical and, likely, emotional pain from his youth—only this time as an adult and this time on his terms."[54]

The two of them had already scripted the scene, agreed on a safe word, and designed a high-quality safety protocol: Darren and Alicia would both slowly undress him, while maintaining steady eye contact; he would then bend over a padded bench designed specifically for this purpose, and invite her to spank him with a belt until he either said their safe word or indicated the completion of the ritual by saying "it's done."[55] The complete experience would last no more than an hour, and a close friend of theirs was to call them one hour and five minutes after the scene had begun to ensure that they were both okay. If they didn't answer, he was to immediately come over to their house and check on them.[56] They told Dr. Ortmann that they had already decided to go through with this experience, with or without him, and would appreciate his willingness to help them integrate whatever came up in the scene.[57]

He agreed. The following Saturday, Darren and Alicia played through the scene exactly as they had planned it. "I don't even remember everything I said," Darren later told Dr. Ortmann. "The words, the cursing, the hatred, the name calling, the *hate*. . . . It all just poured out of me. . . . It was like she'd cleaned out a very deep wound with industrial-strength alcohol. It hurt so badly at the time, but there was no doubt when it was over that the wound would, finally, heal."[58]

In fact, it did. After several months of integration with Dr. Ortmann, Darren eventually even began to forgive his mother: "'I feel sorry for her,' he said one day. 'It's weird but I do. . . . I spent so many years hating her and resenting her. I just don't anymore.'

"'What do you feel?'

"'Pity. Compassion. Forgiveness, I guess. I find myself wondering what kind of childhood she must have had and how sad and ruined a person she became. . . . I spent so many Friday nights in that basement and so much of my adulthood was spent there too. . . . It took a lot of work and a lot of time, but I'm not trapped down in that basement anymore. Not Darren the boy, or Darren the man.' He looked at [Dr. Ortmann] and smiled. He had tears in his eyes. 'We got him out, David.'

"'That we did, Darren. That we did.'"[59]

IN THE HEAT OF THE CRUCIBLE

In the narrative of Darren's journey, we are able to see the power of ritual as a transformative crucible, a space that creates the heat and pressure necessary to draw forth the lost pieces of his psyche.

The process of preparing the ritual reads like the ingredients for an alchemist's potion, the meticulously selected elements required for transformation. To evoke the darkness, there is impact play, a drumbeat down the same somatic pathways where lies the emotional wound. And to contain what may emerge in response, there are elements of the present moment—the relationship and trust between Darren, Alicia, and Dr. Ortmann, and their explicit permission and encouragement for whatever is exorcised by the ritual to become present with them. These elements embody the known and unknown, the conscious and unconscious, and they delineate the ritual boundary to contain that liminal space. It is within this space that what was lost can be conjured back into being, the base elements of the container transmuted to their archetypal roles in the divine play unfolding.

And there lies the threshold, the challenge offered to Darren: the option to *play*—to view the circumstance as a game, equally real and unreal, past and present, friend and enemy all at hand to be met by the entirety of his being, unified in its purpose. His hesitant, skirting stutter is obliterated as the catharsis of expression breaks through the walls that had previously limited him, defining the places he may and may not follow the urge of his heart.

It is through play that we can traverse the darkness and the light to experience the full totality of being. The infinite option, far beyond the fleeting wins and losses we focus on so seriously, is play that invites us to play and continue playing, welcoming all as cocreators alongside us, and all experiences as expressions of divine curiosity seeking itself in the other. Play beckons us forth.

7

Concluding Remarks: On White Rabbits and the Vows of Liberation

As far as I'm concerned, if you're going to make things right and wrong you can never talk about fulfilling your bodhisattva vows.[1]

—PEMA CHÖDRÖN

A land was full of wonder, mystery, and danger. Some say, to survive it, you need to be as mad as a hatter. Which, luckily, I am.[2]

—MAD HATTER, A CHARACTER IN
LEWIS CARROLL'S *ALICE'S ADVENTURES IN WONDERLAND*

INVITATIONS TO THE INFINITE

The previous chapters have provided an understanding of play and games as the underlying fabric of the world, a perspective that offers liberation from the humdrum or obligation. But having recognized this perspective for ourselves, and once we have experienced that freedom, how do we free those who have forgotten they are in prison? Those with no awareness of their voluntary suffering?

This is the foundational premise of *The Game,* a psychological thriller by filmmaker David Fincher, which lays out one possible answer to this question through the case study of a bitter and alienating financier named Nicholas van Orton. In larger-than-life drama, the film draws us into sympathy for his predicament and sweeps us along in the bewildering and ultimately enlightening ride.

If anyone would reject an invitation to play, it would be Nicholas: In one of the movie's first scenes, we watch as he declines every social invitation that his secretary informs him of. And when she wonders aloud why she bothers even telling him, he replies, "If you don't know about society, you don't have the satisfaction of avoiding it."

The only two people who seem to care for him are his brother, Conrad, and his ex-wife, Elizabeth, both of whom he pushes away. And yet, on occasion, he does answer their calls, suggesting a hidden yearning for connection. So, when Conrad sneaks up behind him at a restaurant, squirts him with a spray bottle, and says, "Miss me?" Nicholas replies, "As much as that's possible." And he means it: he really does miss his brother as much as his identity permits; he wouldn't have met with him otherwise, would have simply relegated him to the list of people he has the satisfaction of avoiding.

Given his personality, Nicholas is understandably skeptical when Conrad hands him a gift certificate for a company called Consumer Recreation Services and tells him to "call that number. It'll make your life fun," he insists. "Do you know what that is? Have you seen other people have it?"

Nicholas's tentativeness is justified, for, although he doesn't know it, CRS's sole purpose is to utterly dismantle the scripts of their customers by designing games that unleash them into infinite play. The ice tea that his server spills on him the moment he accepts this invitation, then, is an external reflection of this inner disruption, reflecting back to him the destabilizing volatility he has just taken into his world.

When his ex-wife calls him later that night to wish him a happy birthday, we learn that Nicholas has just turned forty-eight, the same age his father was when he died. "I just thought this might be difficult for you . . . because of your father," she says.

"That's right, he was forty-eight, wasn't he? I hadn't really thought about him till now," he says, lying. For Nicholas is incapable of letting her know that he's been thinking of his father all day, that involuntary reveries from his childhood have drifted in and out of his awareness.

After a while more of curt dialogue, he hangs up the phone and returns to his birthday plans: watching financial news, alone, with a tray of premade dinner and a single glass of champagne. Suddenly, we see a flashback of his father jumping off the roof of their family home, as a young Nicholas, horrified, watches from nearby. And then it all begins to make sense: How an event so traumatic would set a script like his into motion; one that keeps people at a distance, so their abandonment won't hurt as badly; one that obscures his buried feelings of anger, sadness, betrayal, and helplessness beneath an identity of numbness, apathy, deadness, and control. And when people do inevitably leave him, as, ironically, his script demands, his role-bound cynicism prevents him from feeling the attendant desperation.

This is precisely the prison that Nicholas's game is designed to free him from. And it will do so by disrupting, or even inverting, his script at increasing levels of intensity, eliminating the tools he typically uses to regain control, and throwing him continually back onto his own mind and the voluntary nature of its boundaries along the way.

We see this from the first moment he walks into the CRS lobby. For when he takes his invitation out of his pocket and tells the secretary, "I received this," she cuts him off, holds up her finger, and says, "Just a moment"—dismissing him in exactly the same way he dismisses everyone else. A second inversion quickly follows, when he meets Jim Feingold, "VP Engineering," who escorts him into a disheveled office and hands him a bag of Chinese food ("You mind holding that?") as he rifles through a file cabinet. Here, Nicholas is not only dismissed, but put into a service position. A third inversion happens soon after, when Feingold lets him know that the company does "a sort of informal scoring," and that his "slacker" brother Conrad's "numbers are outstanding."

These first few disruptions arouse his curiosity ("admit to yourself that it sounds intriguing") enough to have him agree to fill out CRS's forms and take their psychological evaluation. And when he clicks open his pen to begin with the forms, we see him smile, however faintly, for the first time in the film.

INTO THE INVISIBLE

Later that night, Nicholas "coincidentally" overhears some guys talking about CRS, further piquing his curiosity. And when he asks them what the game is about, one of them answers, cryptically: "You want to know what it is? What it's all about? John, chapter 9, verse 25 . . . 'Whereas once I was blind, now I can see.'"

The reference is apt. Every moment of the game, every scene and script inversion, is meant to awaken his vision to the invisible rules that structure his world, and the voluntary nature of his adherence to them; to the possibility of another world, beyond the boundaries of those rules; and to the subtle details in his environment, any of which may act as a portal to that new reality.

The game does this by bringing Nicholas into contact with the buried feelings and unconscious decisions that arose as a result of his father's death, so that he may dissolve his script by integrating its central wound. This is why the first major scene in his game has him come upon a clown mannequin in his driveway, placed in exactly the same spot his father fell when he died.

When he drags the mannequin into his living room, and pulls a key out of its mouth, he receives the first, and only, overt communication of the game's boundaries—when his television begins to talk to him. "This is your game, Nicholas, and welcome to it," says the newscaster, to Nicholas's astonishment. "I'm here to let you in on a few ground rules. You received the very first key, and others will follow. You'll never know where you'll find them, or how you'll need to use them, so keep your eyes open."

And he does. Since he no longer knows what is or isn't part of the game, Nicholas is forced to take in details that he wouldn't have perceived before. Time seems to move in slow motion, as he notices a deaf couple signing; a janitor unlocking a door; a flight attendant on the telephone; and a man who's run out of toilet paper in the bathroom stall beside him. The boundaries of his reality soften as his attention opens to meet it, meeting a world in which everything and yet nothing is the same.

DOWN THE RABBIT HOLE

Gradually, he starts to alternate between the rules of his script, which are increasingly irrelevant, and the rules of the game, which are unknown and disorienting. For example, when he returns to his usual restaurant, and the same server, Christine, spills a drink on him *again,* he first reacts in the scripted way—by yelling at her and getting her fired. But when the check arrives with a note that says, "Don't let her get away," he leaves that script behind and catches up with her in a dark alley.

His willingness to follow the game's guidance causes a rapid escalation of its intensity. For in the next few moments: A man drops nearly dead in front of them; Nicholas waves down a cop car for help; and paramedics insist he and Christine get into an ambulance, only to abandon them in a dark, empty, underground parking lot.

Not content to sit around in the ambulance, Christine ventures into the darkness in search of a way out. Nicholas follows, deeper into the uncertainty of this reality. For in this exteriorization of his inner landscape, Christine plays the part of the archetypal feminine, whose absence is felt everywhere as a lack of tenderness, intimacy, and the capacity for feeling. After so many years of alienation from this archetype, he has finally found her, alive and in the flesh, and he can't let her get away, not again, not this time. So, as she leads the way, he follows, awakening his natural capacity to see in the dark at every level of abstraction.

Eventually, they find an elevator, only to discover that it isn't working. But when Nicholas tries using the key he'd pulled from the clown's mouth, it turns on and begins to rise—only to stop again moments later, leaving them stranded, without a phone, in the middle of the elevator shaft.

Christine, whom he still doesn't realize is in on the game, then suggests they remove a ceiling tile and climb up to the next floor. "Okay, I'll give you a boost," he says, after much resistance. But she insists that he go first, as she's "not wearing any underwear." And as he moves through this narrow passage, toward an emergence at a higher level— of the building and of consciousness—the feminine is his guide, directing him from below, from her natural proximity to the Erotic power that could and would arouse him from his scriptedness.

His reliance upon this guidance deepens in the next few turns of the game, after a security tripwire forces them to run through a back alley and climb up a scaffolding to escape a pack of attack dogs. Since his own intuition is still too atrophied at this point, she plays the part of that intuition for him, modeling how to perceive and engage with the hidden options in their environment—in real time and under pressure.

AWAKENING TO OPTIONALITY

Upon escaping to Nicholas's office, Christine takes her shirt off and asks if she can use his shower. And he nods, doing his best not to stare at her red bra, as his face turns flush with embarrassed arousal. Life, and with it, color, begins to return to his body, as the Erotic heat between them melts off these first few layers of numbness.

When he gets her a cab ride home, she adds a little more fuel to this fire by confessing that "someone gave me $400 to spill drinks on you as a practical joke. . . . They said, '300,' I said, '4.' They said, 'The guy in the gray flannel suit,' I think I said, 'The attractive guy in the gray flannel suit?'"

Nicholas gently smiles as she rolls up her window and drives off into the night.

With each of these artful flashes of sexuality, she draws him further out of his habitual reality and into the possibility of ecstasy. But this possibility is complicated in the very next scene, when he receives a message from a hotel he's never been to before, informing him that they have his credit card at the front desk. And when he arrives at the hotel, he discovers that the room his card has paid for is littered with drugs, trash, pornography, and blurry Polaroid photos of a woman in a red bra that looks eerily similar to Christine. An ambivalence arises, in which fear, confusion, and rage intermix with the prior tenderness and arousal, forging a potent union of opposites characteristic of true Eros.

And when Nicholas returns to his home, he finds that it is just as destroyed as that hotel room: with graffiti everywhere and loud music blaring over a speaker system in the living room. A folder, which has been jammed into the clown's mouth, holds a paper on which are written the words, "Like my father before me, I choose eternal sleep," along with a forensic photograph of his father laying dead on the ground after his suicide. Another layer of unfelt childhood feelings rise up to the surface, as we witness him tremble with panic and rage.

These feelings are translated into language when Conrad shows up, in the middle of this mess, demands that they drive off the property, and then provokes him into an argument. For in the heat of their shouting match, Conrad yells, "Nobody asked you to play dad!"

To which Nicholas replies, furiously: "No! You *don't* say that! Did I have a choice? Did I have a choice?"

By bringing his awareness to the covert agreements he made in the wake of his father's death, the game directs him to consider this question of choice sincerely, and not just rhetorically. For, in every moment, he does indeed have a choice: as to whether he will let this wound continue to define him, or whether he will release himself from the past and move on.

That CRS is willing to use any means necessary to awaken this optionality becomes clear when he gets into a cab with an apparent psychopath. As the driver speeds through a series of red lights and swerves maniacally down the road, Nicholas, sensing that his life is in danger, begs him to let him out of the car. "Listen," he pleads, "I am a very wealthy man, and whatever they're paying you, I'll double it!"

But the driver responds only with sadistic laughter, as he knows that Nicholas can't throw money at this problem: The only way out is to engage with the game, as if his life were on the line.

And in this case it really seems to be. For when the driver jumps out of the moving cab and sends it hurtling into the bay with Nicholas locked in the back seat, he's forced to innovate immediately. Although the serious mind may see this as a reckless amount of pressure to put someone under, it is in fact the precise amount of pressure he needs for his play instinct to come alive.

We know this, because it works: As the cab sinks deeper into the water, Nicholas asks himself, "If it's a game, if it's a game . . ." And with this simple question, this act of cognitive reappraisal, he moves out of his script enough to notice that the knob to open the window is missing. Remembering that he has just such a knob in his pocket (it was the last key he received), he attaches it to the cab door, opens the window, and swims away to safety.

Uncoincidentally, this near-death experience, and the optionality it awakens in him, causes Nicholas to reflect about his life. For a true awakening to optionality is an awakening at all levels: physical, mental, emotional, and spiritual. Since we never know where life's options might be hiding, we must become alert to the invisible across dimensions, including and especially those interior dimensions that would otherwise obscure our vision. So, when he makes his way home, Nicholas surprises his housekeeper by asking her what his father was like ("All the time I've known you, you've never once asked about him"). And as they talk about his father, he wonders aloud, "How much of him there is in me."

DEATH AND REBIRTH

This disruption of his reality further accelerates when he next encounters Christine again, whose apartment his secretary has managed to track down. When he arrives at her place, he quickly realizes that it is staged: the sinks don't run, the fridge is empty, and the pictures on the shelves are magazine cutouts. When he confronts her about the staging, she whispers to him that they can't talk there, that CRS is listening through the smoke alarm.

Things escalate fast, as an enraged Nicholas begins to scream and thrash at the smoke alarm, causing armed shooters to jump out of a van and shoot at them both from the street. And though he had initially come to question her about the Polaroid images ("What makes you think this is me?" / "The bra, the red bra . . ."), Nicholas finds himself following her, again, as they escape from the apartment and drive away from the machine gunfire of the CRS agents. He tries to ditch her on the side of the road, but she reminds him, "You don't have a choice. Nobody else is going to tell you what's going on!"

And he knows that she's right. So, as they drive off together to a cabin outside the city, he asks her to confess everything she knows about the game.

At this point, Nicholas has no idea what to believe. But he listens attentively as she tells him that the game is a con, designed only to drain his bank accounts. "You took their tests, handwriting, voice samples, psych info. . . . They used it all to figure out your passwords." And when he calls his bank in Zurich to check the balance on his account, he discovers, to his horror, that it is empty.

The emotional intensity of this shock only serves to further the Erotic tension between them—a tension that has little to do with who she really is, and everything to do with the archetype she represents for him. For just like his inner feminine, he loves her, but also hates her; he wants to trust her, but he knows she's untrustworthy; and when she reveals to him things that no one else will, he doesn't know which of them are lies.

With every moment of her seduction, Christine calls him deeper into intimacy with this part of himself: With that feminine soul, whose Erotic intelligence combines both tenderness and aggression, truth and falsehood, creation and destruction in one daemonic unity. For the "soul is a woman," writes Rilke, articulating an intuition that Jung later confirmed in his years of clinical practice. And Christine is willing to play the part of that soul, to hold its projection until he's ready to hold it in himself.

This representation of his feminine soul-image intensifies when they arrive at his cabin in the woods. As he sips on the tea she has prepared for him, Nicholas's perception starts to take on a psychedelic quality. He falls to the ground in the stupor of this intoxication, his glance drifts first to the tea, and then to Christine, who is now hovering over him in all her terrible beauty. "Cellular calls can be intercepted," she says. "All those calls you made? B of A, France, you were talking to us. You filled in the blanks: access codes and passwords. . . . We have it now, so we're done. Bye, Nicholas."

At this point, every trace of her human personality has dissolved into the numinosity of the archetype. No longer Christine, she has become Circe, the Homeric goddess whose potions turn men into swine; the goddess Joseph Campbell calls "the erotic impulse absolute."[3] For "the Great Goddess of the night, as ruler of the unconscious," writes psychologist Erich Neumann, "is the goddess not only of poisons but of sleep . . . because seizure in large part presupposes an exclusion of the normal daytime consciousness."[4]

That she is, in the symbol system of this ritual playground, the goddess not only of poisons and sleep but also of life and death is made clear in the next scene, where we see Nicholas awaken from his blackout in an open tomb of a Mexican graveyard. Having been left for dead with no cash or identification (for his old identity has evaporated, and with it the ability to throw money at his problems), he sells his father's watch to bribe his way back into the country, and hitches a ride to San Francisco to find his ex-wife—literally the last person in the world that he can trust.

When he finds her, we discover that this death-and-rebirth ritual has granted him the clarity to recognize his feelings, as well as the maturity to take ownership of his impact on others. "I'm sorry, Liz," he tells her.

"You know, I've been thinking the last couple of days, I've had some spare time, and I wanted to tell you that I understand why you left me. And I know that I resented it. I want to apologize to you for shutting you out, for not being there. And I hope that you can forgive me."

She replies, "There's nothing to forgive."

Despite the outer conditions of his life, then, which by all measures appear to be an unmitigated catastrophe, his inner life has clearly begun to flourish. The tenderness that before lived only as a possibility has now become available to him as a lived experience. And, as is only natural, the emergence of this tenderness coincides with the emergence of his healthy aggression: for the Erotic power he has now integrated unifies all opposites, allowing him to flexibly respond to the demands of the moment by bringing forth whichever energy is most resonant for the scene.

So, when he sees Jim Feingold on a TV ad, and concludes he must be an actor, it doesn't take Nicholas long to track the man down and demand that he lead him to the CRS office. When Jim tries to protest, telling him that it would be extremely dangerous to go there, Nicholas pulls out a gun and says: "I don't think you understand. Right now *I* am extremely dangerous." Having set aside the finite goals of money and security, he has become willing to risk his life to play toward a horizon he can neither see nor even conceptualize—toward the mystery that lies at the center of the game.

With Feingold as his guide, he enters the CRS office and spots Christine sitting at a table with the taxi driver. It doesn't take long for security to notice him, and as the guards open fire with machine guns, he chases her, pistol in hand, toward the rooftop of the building. When they make it to the roof—just the two of them, with the door shut—he unleashes the full explosiveness of his rage, threatening to kill her if she doesn't get her boss up there. For he still doesn't realize that this, too, has been choreographed, masterfully designed to draw him past the point of no return.

"They don't care about me," she cries out in desperation. "They'll let me die. You're not in a position to threaten anyone!" But as her attention moves to his gun, she begins to panic. "Wait a minute, where'd you get that, that gun, that's not an automatic," she says, picking up her walkie-talkie and telling her team, "We've got a real goddamn gun up here." She then begs Nicholas to put the gun down, telling him that all of this is fake—it's just a part of the game.

But he doesn't believe her, not now, not anymore. As their back and forth escalates, she says: "You're about to make the biggest mistake of your life. . . . They're waiting on the other side of that door with champagne. Nicholas, please, God dammit. . . . Conrad's there, it's your birthday party!"

But as the door to the rooftop begins to open, Nicholas fires his gun—and hits Conrad, who is holding a bottle of champagne, "killing" him on the spot. Christine and Jim then rush over to treat the gunshot wound ("How'd you let this get so out of hand?"), as Nicholas walks over to the ledge of the building in a daze and then jumps. As he falls to his death, scenes from his childhood, scenes with his father, flash across his mind's eye. Having killed his brother, the person his script was meant to protect, Nicholas actualizes the darkest, most painful recess of his psyche—the formative wound of his father's suicide—and delivers his body over entirely to that experience. In doing so, he comes to know, from the inside out, what could have driven his father to do such a thing.

His dive into this central trauma, then, gives him the experiential empathy to loosen its grip on him once and for all. It is a leap out of the boundaries of his known reality, a death of his scripted identity by way of an inner resolution of the incident that started it all.

Falling through the glass ceiling of the building beneath him, he lands, to his bewilderment, on a large, inflatable breakfall at the center of a party—with everyone he knows in attendance. Conrad then appears, with fake blood smeared across his white tuxedo, says, "Happy birthday, Nickie," and holds up a shirt that reads, "I was drugged and left for dead in Mexico—and all I got was this stupid T-shirt." And as it dawns on him that Conrad is fine, that all of this was just a game, Nicholas begins to sob in his brother's arms, who whispers that he "had to do something. . . . You were becoming such an asshole."

COMMUNITAS AND CONTINUATION DESIRE

His birthday, then, becomes a celebration of the courage and vulnerability it took to free himself, as well as an affirmation of the new and true identity that has emerged. For one of the most masterful elements of the game is that it enrolls his entire community into affecting his transformation, allowing him to organically renegotiate his relationships with each of them along the way. It is only natural, then, that when he dies to his old self and is reborn to his true nature, all of his loved ones—and they are now capable of being loved ones—should be surrounding and witnessing him. Suddenly, every shock to his identity, every terrifying turn, is seen for what it truly was: an act of unwavering devotion to the spirit that was imprisoned in him, the spirit that his game was designed to set free.

After greeting, embracing, and apologizing to his loved ones, Nicholas's mind turns to Christine—the primary catalyst of his transformation—whom he manages to catch just as she's getting into a cab outside the party.

"So, you, um, catching a plane?" he asks, no longer needing someone to tell him not to let her get away.

"Yeah, we have a gig starting next week in Australia," And when he asks her if she'd like to get dinner sometime, she ponders for a moment, before asking if he'd like to get coffee with her at the airport instead. As he looks off into the distance, with a faint smile on his face, the movie fades to black.

Because that's how it always goes, in the end: Having left the finite world, with all its suffocating seriousness, and entered the infinite game, there is nothing he would rather do than continue on his play through the liberation of others. It is no coincidence that Christine (we learn that her name is really Claire) is the one to invite him into this continuation. Having followed her to his own soul, he would now follow her anywhere—into the expanse of this open-ended mystery, into the living vow to awaken the others, startling them back to the truth of who they are: free players in a divine playground called life.

AT PLAY IN THE WORLD

We may finish a viewing of *The Game* with two takeaways. The first is the wish for some CRS agents to burst into our humdrum life, disrupting the habits and scripts we have used to isolate ourselves from life, to be liberated into the wild world of play. Or, second, we can take it upon ourselves to begin the play. There are two kinds of people in the world, party goers and party-throwers and, having reached this far in the book, you have the tools and inspiration you need to throw a great party.

Katie, when I met her, wasn't having much fun. She was a middle-aged woman living in the hills outside San Francisco in an upscale neighborhood. She had everything—the perfect life. She was married to a well-known CEO in the entertainment industry and hosted dinner parties at their pristine mansion on a weekly basis. Katie was the perfect wife, she looked and played the part. She was petite, thin, with blond hair and blue eyes—that Farrah Fawcett–variety of American beauty, thoroughbred to the bone. She and her husband were the right match for each other, both intelligent and successful. She had all the right mannerisms and credentials. In short, she was bored, acting out her role in the perfect dull and lifeless world that had been constructed around her.

Beneath the layer of composure was a passion and curiosity for life that had gone untapped. It was a crossroads moment. She could have continued the life she'd been living and been completely successful. But she also had a longing to know and discover parts of herself that had been lying dormant in her soul.

INVITATION

When we met, Katie was intrigued and ready to break open the doorway that would lead to something new. At first, it was a slow process getting to know her, and her getting to know us, waking up to the sense that there was something more to be had just beyond the veil. As her desire became clear, we offered an invitation to participate in a game designed just for her. This was the first move of the game.

Katie's game would be an overt, formal game with a set time and would take place in various places throughout San Francisco. Like all games, it would be constructed of a goal and rules, a feedback system, and voluntary participation. The goal of the game would be to escort her into her involuntary state, the aspect of her being that yearned for touch and play. Katie was always in control and on top of her game, a natural leader—even her career was in serving others. She was always the organizer and caretaker, but so rarely had the experience of letting go and being out of control, of having someone else handle her with the kind of love, care, and precision that she had for others.

THE CIRCLE

We had done our research, but to be even more explicit, we drew up a questionnaire for her to let us know exactly how she liked to play. It was not so far off from the evaluations and surveys completed by Nicholas at the CRS headquarters. You have to learn someone so intimately to meet them in their covert games and deliver their hidden desires. We were to infiltrate as secret agents deep enough into her psyche to disrupt the routine patterns of navigating the world and liberate the sense within her that had been trapped for too long. But far from the dramatic and life-threatening measures taken within the safety of fiction, we can lean on the power of Eros to entice her. We offered her a survey of a dozen aspects of experience, from fantasy to introspection, confrontation to creativity, and had her rate each by the amount of pleasure she derived. When we saw her rating spike at music and confrontation, her fears around money and her desire for touch, then the shape of the game began to take form.

It's not enough to have a general sense of what someone likes and dislikes, particularly when purposefully venturing into that intimate, liminal space. Just as in the example of Darren's BDSM experience, we needed to draw the boundaries of our ritual circle, to set the rules for our game. What were her specific boundaries? The conditions she brought into the play? From details as rote as a list of allergies to her specific fears that arise in anticipation of the experience, we wanted to know them all so that we could handle any detail and be conscious of any obstacle that might otherwise interrupt the flow of the game.

Implicitly, we would have an empathetic sense of her joy and excitement in being a part of the game and would keep a consistent person with her to guide Katie and evaluate how she was doing with her experience. We created an explicit feedback system of safe words to use through the experience; "green" for go, "yellow" for slow down, and "red" to ask for the play to stop.

THE PLAYERS

The cast came together from volunteers who had played these kinds of games before and were excited to be a part of the fun. We had twenty-four hours to devise the plan, write the parts, coordinate the behind-the-scene moves, write the music, find the costumes. . . . It could have been a tiresome list, but this is play for the players in all the roles, marked by fun, a diminished sense of self-consciousness, time dilation, optionality. All of these elements contribute to the autotelic experience that defines play; the reason we choose to play and continue playing, enjoying each inspiration that emerges and the challenge it brings with it as a call to move deeper and deeper into the flow of the game. Hidden talents emerge, roles and responsibilities organize themselves organically, and coincidences arrive on angel wings to bring it all together.

It would be a whole cast of men and women Katie had never met before and who had never met her, but who were joyously committed to bringing a new player into the infinite game.

THE PLAY

I met her at a café. We had arranged this in advance, nothing as cinematic as anything in *The Game*, but there was little need for it. Her body shivered with excitement for the evening, her anticipation of the unknown fun that lay ahead already enlivening her cheeks, her eyes, her smile. She was glowing. Every detail of the space became full of potential to her—was the waiter in on it? The couple that just came through the door? We finished our tea, and I wished her well on her adventure, letting her know that I would see her again afterward.

Katie walked outside to be met by an angel, Marya, a woman she had never met before but who glowed with that same excitement Katie felt. She would escort Katie through the play, holding her hand in the darkness. They began their walk to their first stop and, along the way, seemingly random strangers gifted flowers to her, bringing beauty to the play.

They arrived at a church in the middle of service, Marya whisking Katie up to the choir loft to join in the hymns and prayer songs, the first of several musical offerings. As they turned to go to their next destination, a patron offered her a coffee and pastries.

They continued through the streets of San Francisco, flowers and snacks in hand, until Marya spotted a Peruvian shaman offering readings on the sidewalk. How could Katie resist? Her fortune told, a blessing given, and his insistence that she must remember her *alma*, Spanish for "soul," if she were to gain access to the sensuality she desired.

A street person came up to them asking if they had any food. Was she a part of the play? In either case, Katie had the coffee and pastry and was happy to share. It was a joy to circulate, to empty her fullness and fill what was empty. Moments later, they passed an anxious, fumbling man on the street, a friend of Marya's, on his way to a date he was clearly excited about.

"Have my flowers!" Katie joyously offered, learning the currency of this new world.

Refreshingly emptied, Katie and her angel continued on, cutting through Union Square. But there were more hands, more requests from dirty faces, and the two of them had given away the few things they had and were traveling light. This touched a fear of Katie's, the fear of losing everything—her husband losing his job, the finances falling through, ending up trapped in a life like the people she saw on the streets of the city. But then a song she recognized began playing from the boombox on the ground, something incongruous to the whole scene, and suddenly the mob around them jumped up to dance along to the 1970s favorite of hers from *Dirty Dancing*. Those who were actually homeless pointed at the scene unfolding, laughing along with the joy of it, another wild night in the city. She felt grateful for the players but maybe identified even more with a woman by the shopping cart and the men holding their drinks in paper bags, all part of the audience as the performance unfolded. Their joy was her joy and in that moment, she felt her money anxieties relax as the separation between them dissolved.

The performance was ending, but Marya was already whisking her into a taxi, off to their next location. When they arrived at the gate, they were asked for a password. "Alma," Katie knew to say intuitively, following the shaman's advice. Once inside, a massage did indeed bring the sensuality that had been missing from her life, that the spa days she had gone to had not been able to touch. But here, in the midst of play, an integral part of her adventure, her body relaxed and opened to receive the touch she'd missed.

One last stop, a small theater. The doorman gave a nod to Marya and ushered them inside to where we were sitting, waiting for Katie to join us. We were the only ones in the theater, and the spotlight seemed as much on her as on the curtains that drew open to reveal the show. A musical, cast by the characters that had lit her way on the path to this culmination, showing the life of two different women, similar on the outside but lit by entirely different energies within. Light and dark, they admired each other, each changed for the better by coming to know each other. And as the dream of the musical broke, Katie was shown a character of herself on the stage, now full of life, excitement, turned on to find a character of her husband and ravish him as the full cast—street people, shaman, masseuse, the anxious boyfriend holding the bouquet, and more—filled the stage in song.

As it ended, Katie burst from her seat in applause and gratitude big enough to fill the whole theater. Indeed, from stage to seats, every person shouting and clapping, the gift and gratitude shared in full circulation.

ACROSS THE THRESHOLD

To gather after and share frames of favorite moments from the entire production felt like a reunion. Katie was alive and electric, full of the life that comes from play. The revelations of what had transpired on either side of the roles, from the cast or Katie, the gleeful initiate, were now met with laughter rejoined. But that feeling, the expectant uncertainty, the willingness to be called and follow the ride on which you are beckoned—that is as possible here as it was in the scripted game.

As the frames came to a close, there was one more destination for the evening, dinner with her husband. A playmate to be invited into the game, to share that same liberation into the infinite fun of play.

Acknowledgments

Dear Reader,

Since you have just concluded your journey through this book, I need to acknowledge the gifted writer behind the words you have read on its pages.

While the foundational concepts of this book, anchored in the Eros Sutras on Play and Liberation as well as my decades dedicated to exploring play, are mine, his literary finesse breathed life into them. His eloquence conveys my ideas beautifully, and the brilliance often found between these lines belongs to him.

Life, mirroring the dance of play, throws unexpected turns. We live in a culture that believes in guilt by association, and when storms of controversy arose around me, he made the choice not to be connected to this work.

I believe play is the path, the practice, and the result of liberation. What we consider trivial is of the highest order, but the seeming reality of problems hijacks the nonrational quality of genius that always occurs in play, in the autotelic.

May this book further the play agenda in the world. May all who contributed to its creation reap great fruit from the process. And may all of us find the field of play and the ground of joy.

And while he remains unnamed, know that my writer friend's presence is felt in every page. My gratitude remains.

Notes

CHAPTER ONE

1. Hugo Rahner, *Man at Play* (Chestnut Ridge, NY: Herder and Herder Publishing, 1967), 125.
2. William S. Sax, *The Gods at Play: Lila in South Asia* (Oxford, UK: Oxford University Press, 1995), 38.
3. Kinsley, David R. *The Divine Player: A Study of Krishna Lila* (Delhi, India: Motilal Banarsidass, 1979), 263–264.
4. Rahner, Hugo. *Man at Play* (New York: Herder and Herder, 1979), 89–90.
5. Anuradha, "Brahma Creates the Universe," March 6, 2013, All About Hinduism, https://www.allabouthinduism.info/2013/03/06/brahma-creates/.
6. Graham M. Schweig, *Dance of Divine Love: India's Classic Sacred Love Story: The Rasa Lila of Krishna* (Princeton, NJ: Princeton University Press, 2005), 38.
7. Jane McGonigal, *Reality Is Broken: Why Games Make Us Better and How They Can Change the World* (New York: Penguin Press, 2011), 77.
8. McGonigal, *Reality Is Broken*, 78.
9. McGonigal, *Reality Is Broken*, 79.
10. Schweig, *Dance of Divine Love*, 67–70.
11. Sax, *Gods at Play*, 38.
12. Sax, *Gods at Play*, 38.
13. Gopal K. Gupta, *Maya in the Bhagavata Purana: Human Suffering and Divine Play* (Oxford, UK: Oxford University Press, 2020), 97.
14. Lewis Hyde, *Trickster Makes This World: Mischief, Myth, and Art* (Edinburgh, UK: Canongate Books, 2008), 71.
15. Hyde, *Trickster Makes This World*, 285.
16. Brown, Stuart L. *Play: How It Shapes the Brain, Opens the Imagination, and Invigorates the Soul* (New York: Avery, 2009), p. 75.

CHAPTER TWO

1. Stephen Nachmanovitch, *Free Play: Improvisation in Life and Art* (New York: Penguin Books, 1991), 42.

2. Gordon M. Burghardt, *The Genesis of Animal Play: Testing the Limits* (Cambridge, MA: MIT Press, 2005), 45.

3. E. O. Wilson, *Sociobiology: The New Synthesis* (Cambridge, MA: Belknap Press, 1975), 45.

4. Stuart Brown and Christopher Vaughan, *Play: How It Shapes the Brain, Opens the Imagination, and Invigorates the Soul* (New York: Avery [Penguin Books], 2009), 33.

5. Johan Huizinga, *Homo Ludens: A Study of the Play-Element of Culture* (Mansfield Center, CT: Martino Publishing, 2014 [originally published in Dutch, 1938]), 13.

6. "play" (v.) (the etymology of "play"), Online Etymology Dictionary, accessed August 5, 2023, https://www.etymonline.com/word/play.

7. Victor Turner, *From Ritual to Theatre: The Human Seriousness of Play* (Cambridge, MA: PAJ Publications, 2001), 33.

8. Huizinga, *Homo Ludens,* 39.

9. Huizinga, *Homo Ludens,* 39.

10. Huizinga, *Homo Ludens,* 40.

11. "play," https://www.etymonline.com/word/play.

12. Huizinga, *Homo Ludens,* 39.

13. Robson Bello, "Presence and Possibilities of Play?" May 4, 2023, USC Shoah Foundation, https://sfi.usc.edu/news/2023/05/35186-presence-and-possibilities-play.

14. Jalal al-Din Rumi, *The Essential Rumi*, trans., Coleman Barks and John Moyne (New York: HarperOne, 2004), 18.

15. David R. Kinsley, *The Divine Player: A Study of Krsna Lila* (Delhi, India: Motilal Banarsidass, 1979), 101.

16. Rumi, *The Essential Rumi,* 18.

17. Louis Markos, *From Achilles to Christ: Why Christians Should Read the Pagan Classics* (New York: Harper Classics, 2007), 118.

18. Turner, *From Ritual to Theatre,* 17.

19. Turner, *From Ritual to Theatre,* 17.

20. Turner, *From Ritual to Theatre,* 17.

21. Turner, *From Ritual to Theatre,* 17.

22. Huizinga, *Homo Ludens,* 31.

23. Steven Kotler, *The Rise of Superman: Decoding the Science of Ultimate Human Performance* (New York: Houghton Mifflin Harcourt, 2014), 144.

24. Kotler, *Rise of Superman,* 101.

25. Kotler, *Rise of Superman*, 102.
26. Huizinga, *Homo Ludens*, 43.
27. Huizinga, *Homo Ludens*, 33.
28. Huizinga, *Homo Ludens*, 43.
29. Huizinga, *Homo Ludens*, 43.
30. Turner, *From Ritual to Theatre*, 41.
31. Brown, *Play*, 126.
32. Brown, *Play*, 16.
33. Mihaly Csikszentmihalyi, *Flow: The Psychology of Optimal Experience* (New York: Harper, 1991), 145–46.
34. James P. Carse, *Finite and Infinite Games: A Vision of Life and Possibilities* (New York: Ballantine Publishing, 1985), 3.
35. Nachmanovitch, *Free Play*, 88.
36. Brown, *Play*, 28.
37. Brown, *Play*, 28.
38. Rollo May, *Love and Will* (New York: W. W. Norton & Company, 1969), 75.
39. Nachmanovitch, *Free Play*, 72.
40. Csikszentmihalyi, *Flow*, 62.
41. Kotler, *Rise of Superman*, 49.
42. Kotler, *Rise of Superman*, 49.
43. Kotler, *Rise of Superman*, 49.
44. Ilan Goldberg, Michal Harel, and Rafael Malach, "When the Brain Loses Its Self: Prefrontal Inactivation during Sensorimotor Process," *Neuron*, vol. 50, issue 2 (2006): 329–39, https://doi.org/10.1016/j.neuron.2006.03.015.
45. Kotler, *Rise of Superman*, 49.
46. Kotler, *Rise of Superman*, 54.
47. Nachmanovitch, *Free Play*, 399.
48. Nassim Nicholas Taleb, *Antifragile: Things That Gain from Disorder* (New York: Random House, 2012), 188.
49. Taleb, *Antifragile*, 189.
50. Microbiology Society, "The History of Antibiotics," Members Outreach Resources, accessed August 5, 2023, https://microbiologysociety.org/members-outreach-resources/outreach-resources/antibiotics-unearthed/antibiotics-and-antibiotic-resistance/the-history-of-antibiotics.html#:~:text=Alexander%20Fleming%20was%2C%20it%20seems,he%20had%20accidentally%20left%20uncovered.
51. François Jacob, "Evolution and Tinkering," June 10, 1977, *Science*, vol. 196, number 4295, 4, https://web.mit.edu/~tkonkle/www/BrainEvolution/Meeting9/Jacob%201977%20Science.pdf.
52. Jacob, "Evolution and Tinkering," 5.
53. Hyde, *Trickster Makes This World*, 318.

54. Sax, *Gods at Play*, 57.

55. Sax, *Gods at Play*, 57.

56. Mihaly Csikszentmihalyi, *Creativity: Flow and the Psychology of Discovery and Invention* (New York: HarperCollins, 1996), 64.

57. Rainer Maria Rilke, *Rilke on Love and Other Difficulties* (New York: W. W. Norton and Company, 1994), 31.

58. *Encyclopedia Britannica.* "jinni," accessed April 27, 2023. https://www.britannica.com/topic/jinni.

59. Stephen A. Diamond, *Anger, Madness, and the Daimonic: The Psychological Genesis of Violence, Evil, and Creativity* (New York: State University of New York Press, 1995), 20.

60. Julia Cameron, *The Artist's Way: A Spiritual Path to Higher Creativity* (New York: Jeremy P. Tarcher, 1995), 187.

61. Cameron, *The Artist's Way*, 75.

62. "Michelangelo: Paintings, Sculptures, Biography," Michelangelo.org, accessed August 4, 2023, https://www.michelangelo.org/michelangelo-quotes.jsp.

63. Elizabeth Gilbert, "Your Elusive Creative Genius," 2009, TED Talk, https://www.youtube.com/watch?v=86x-u-tz0MA.

64. Huizinga, *Homo Ludens*, 158.

CHAPTER THREE

1. Robert Mitchell, "A Theory of Play," *Interpretation and Explanation in the Study of Animal Behavior.* Marc Bekoff and Dale Jamieson, eds. (Boulder: Westview Press, 2019), 197–227.

2. Aldous Huxley, *Collected Essays* (New York: Bantam Books, 1964), 83.

3. Kinsley, *The Divine Player*, 4.

4. Brown, *Play*, 29.

5. Burghardt, *Genesis of Animal Play*, 294, 321, 362.

6. Hyde, *Trickster Makes This World*, 21.

7. Hyde, *Trickster Makes This World*, 22.

8. Paul Shepard, *The Others: How Animals Made Us Human* (Washington, DC: Island Press, 1997), 16.

9. Shepard, *The Others*, 16.

10. Shepard, *The Others*, 16.

11. Lynne Isbell, *The Fruit, the Tree, and–Serpent: Why We See So Well* (Cambridge, MA: Harvard University Press, 2009), 146.

12. Isbell, *The Fruit, the Tree*, 146.

13. Isbell, *The Fruit, the Tree*, 148.

14. Isbell, *The Fruit, the Tree*, 151, 153.

15. Terence McKenna, *Mushrooms, Evolution, and the Millennium*, September 8, 1991, *Terence Talks*, transcript 3, https://www.youtube.com/watch?v=z5xfjjJJ-_I&t=1872s.

16. Shepard, *The Others*, 18.

17. McKenna, *Mushrooms, Evolution, and the Millennium*, transcript 4.

18. McKenna, *Mushrooms, Evolution, and the Millennium*.

19. Terence McKenna, *Food of the Gods: The Search for the Original Tree of Knowledge* (London: Ebury Publishing, 2010), 27.

20. McKenna, *Food of the Gods*, 25.

21. McKenna, *Mushrooms, Evolution, and the Millennium*, transcript 5.

22. McKenna, *Food of the Gods*, 26.

23. Gregory Curtis, *The Cave Painters* (New York: Knopf, 2006).

24. Bruce Rimmell, "The Bird Man of Lascaux," March 20, 2015, Archaic Visions, https://www.visionaryartexhibition.com/archaic-visions/the-bird-man-of-lascaux#:~:text=The%20notion%20that%20the%20cave,become%20a%20kind%20of%20dogma.

25. Euripides, "Bacchae," *Electra, Phoenician Women, Bacchae, and Iphigenia at Aulis* (Indianapolis, IN: Hackett Publishing, 2011) 183.

26. Burghardt, *Genesis of Animal Play*, 8.

27. Shepard, *The Others*, 84–85.

28. Jennifer Ackerman, *The Bird Way: A New Look at How Birds Talk, Work, Play, Parent, and Think* (New York: Penguin, 2020), 146, 156.

29. Marc Bekoff, ed., *Animal Play: Evolutionary, Comparative and Ecological Perspectives* (Cambridge, UK: Cambridge University Pres, 2009), 34.

30. Ackerman, *The Bird Way*, 152–53, 166.

31. Ackerman, *The Bird Way*, 146.

32. Bekoff, *Animal Play*, 36.

33. For example: Bekoff, *Animal Play*, 27; Brown, *Play*, 16.

34. Brown, *Play*, 30.

35. Burghardt, *Genesis of Animal Play*, 46.

36. McKenna, *Food of the Gods*, 41.

37. Bekoff, *Animal Play*, 28.

38. Daniel Dombrowski, *Divine Beauty: The Aesthetics of Charles Hartshorne* (Nashville, TN: Vanderbilt University Press, 2004), 59.

39. Dombrowski, *Divine Beauty*, 64.

40. Burghardt, *Genesis of Animal Play*, 365.

41. Dombrowski, *Divine Beauty*, 66.

42. Dombrowski, *Divine Beauty*, 67.

43. Burghardt, *Genesis of Animal Play*, 265.

44. Dombrowski, *Divine Beauty*, 60.

45. Bekoff, *Animal Play*, 197.

46. Bekoff, *Animal Play*, 197.
47. Bekoff, *Animal Play*, 38.
48. Bekoff, *Animal Play*, 41.
49. Bekoff, *Animal Play*, 41.
50. Shepard, *The Others*, 27.
51. Burghardt, *Genesis of Animal Play*, 78.
52. Burghardt, *Genesis of Animal Play*, 396.
53. Brown, *Play*, 33.
54. Burghardt, *Genesis of Animal Play*, 97.
55. Brown, *Play*, 34.
56. Brown, *Play*, 36.
57. Burghardt, *Genesis of Animal Play*, 394.
58. Carl Gustav Jung, *The Black Books*, vol. 1 (New York: W. W. Norton, 2020), 18.
59. Carl Gustav Jung, *Memories, Dreams, Reflections*, ed. Aniela Jaffe, trans. Clara Winston (New York: Vintage Books, 1989), 209.
60. Jung, *Memories, Dreams, Reflections*, 213.
61. Jung, *Memories, Dreams, Reflections*, 213.
62. Jung, *The Black Books*, vol. 1, 37–38.
63. Carl Gustav Jung, *Liber Novus* (a.k.a. *The Red Book*) (New York: W. W. Norton, 2009), epigraph.
64. Richard Erdoes and Alfonso Ortiz, *American Indian Trickster Tales* (New York: Penguin Books, 1999), 63.
65. Erdoes and Ortiz, *American Indian Trickster Tales,* 64.
66. Hyde, *Trickster Makes This World*, 20.
67. Hyde, *Trickster Makes This World*, 20, 22.
68. Brown, *Play*, 55.
69. Brown, *Play*, 52–53.
70. Brown, *Play*, 55.
71. Hyde, *Trickster Makes This World*, 43.
72. Brown, *Play*, 55.
73. Brown, *Play*, 55–56.
74. Norman Doidge, *The Brain that Changes Itself: Stories of Personal Triumph from the Frontiers of Brain Science* (New York: Penguin Books, 2007), xvii.
75. Doidge, *The Brain That Changes Itself,* 20.
76. Doidge, *The Brain That Changes Itself,* 21.
77. Doidge, *The Brain That Changes Itself,* 21.
78. Doidge, *The Brain That Changes Itself,* 22.
79. Brown, *Play*, 31.
80. Ackerman, *The Bird Way*, 165.
81. Ackerman, *The Bird Way*, 186.

82. Brown, *Play*, 94.
83. Brown, *Play*, 94.
84. Brown, *Play*, 95.
85. Brown, *Play*, 96.
86. Brown, *Play*, 99–100.
87. Bekoff, *Animal Play*, 177.
88. Burghardt, *Genesis of Animal Play*, 91.
89. Burghardt, *Genesis of Animal Play*, 92.
90. Ackerman, *The Bird Way*, 185.
91. Ackerman, *The Bird Way*, 170.
92. Bekoff, *Animal Play*, 128.
93. Burghardt, *Genesis of Animal Play*, 90.
94. Bekoff, *Animal Play*, 174.
95. Ackerman, *The Bird Way*, 165.
96. John Danaher, interview with Lex Fridman, "The Path to Mastery in Jiu Jitsu," podcast audio, May 9, 2021, *Lex Fridman Podcast*, episode 182, http://www .LexFridman.com/John-Danaher.
97. Danaher, "The Path to Mastery in Jiu Jitsu," ep. 182.
98. Brown, *Play*, 21–22.
99. Burghardt, *Genesis of Animal Play*, 405.

CHAPTER FOUR

1. Hermann Hesse, *The Glass Bead Game*, trans. Clara Winston and Richard Winston (New York: Henry Holt and Company, 2002), 396 (note: Also published under the title *Magister Ludi*).
2. Hesse, *The Glass Bead Game*, 188.
3. W. Timothy Gallwey, *The Inner Game of Tennis: The Classic Guide to the Mental Side of Peak Performance* (New York: Random House Publishing, 2010), 103–104.
4. McGonigal, *Reality Is Broken*, 30.
5. Huizinga, *Homo Ludens*, 12.
6. McGonigal, *Reality Is Broken*, 29.
7. McGonigal, *Reality Is Broken,* 286.
8. Gallwey, *The Inner Game of Tennis*, 125.
9. Phil Jackson, *Eleven Rings: The Soul of Success* (New York: Penguin Press, 2013), 108.
10. Jackson, *Eleven Rings*, 109.
11. Nachmanovitch, *Free Play*, 25.
12. Josh Waitzkin, *The Art of Learning: An Inner Journey to Optimal Performance* (New York: Simon and Schuster, 2007), 76.

13. Eric Weil, Richard Giulianotti, Peter Christopher Alegi, Jack Rollin, Bernard Joy, "football." *Encyclopedia Britannica*, accessed July 28, 2023, https://www.britannica.com/sports/football-soccer.

14. Sam Sheridan, *The Fighter's Mind: Inside the Mental Game* (New York: Grove Atlantic Inc., 2010), x.

15. Sheridan, *The Fighter's Mind*, x.

16. Leon Gast, dir., *When We Were Kings*, 1996. PolyGram Filmed Entertainment. Documentary available on Prime Video.

17. Gast, *When We Were Kings*, 1996.

18. Gast, *When We Were Kings*, 1996.

19. McGonigal, *Reality Is Broken*, 287.

20. McGonigal, *Reality Is Broken*, 30.

21. McGonigal, *Reality Is Broken*, 30.

22. Kotler, *The Rise of Superman*, 115.

23. Kotler, *The Rise of Superman*, 114.

24. Csikszentmihalyi, *Flow*, 41.

25. R. Keither Sawyer, *Group Genius: The Power of Creative Collaboration* (New York: Basic Books/Hatchette Book Group, 2017), 64.

26. Sawyer, *Group Genius,* 177.

27. Sawyer, *Group Genius,* 178.

28. Sawyer, *Group Genius,* 177.

29. Csikszentmihalyi, *Flow*, 56.

30. Jane McGonigal, *SuperBetter: The Power of Living Gamefully* (Washington, DC: National Geographic Books, 2016), 103.

31. McGonigal, *SuperBetter*, 100.

32. 8th Garchen Rinpoche, *Guru Stories*, Part 3, "Invincible Courage and Love: Life-Threatening Bravery in a Chinese Jail and Root Guru, Dzogchen Master, Khenpo Munsel," October 25, 2021, https://dakinitranslations.com/2021/10/25/invincible-courage-and-love-life-threatening-bravery-in-a-chinese-jail-and-root-guru-dzogchen-master-khenpo-munsel-guru-stories-part-3-by-8th-garchen-rinpoche/.

33. Garchen Rinpoche, *Guru Stories.*

34. Garchen Rinpoche, *Guru Stories.*

35. Garchen Rinpoche, *Guru Stories.*

36. Garchen Rinpoche, *Guru Stories.*

37. Maylon Hanold, *World Sports: A Reference Handbook* (Santa Barbara, CA: ABC-CLIO Publishing, 2012), 142.

38. Waitzkin, *The Art of Learning*, 12.

39. Sheridan, *The Fighter's Mind*, 199.

40. Josh Waitzkin, interview with Tim Ferriss, podcast audio, *The Tim Ferriss Show,* July 22, 2014, https://www.youtube.com/watch?v=LYaMtGuCgm8

41.   Waitzkin, *The Art of Learning*, 212.

42.   Waitzkin, *The Art of Learning*, 213.

43.   Kotler and Wheal, Stealing Fire, 10.

44.   McGonigal, SuperBetter, 67.

45.   McGonigal, SuperBetter, 67.

46.   McGonigal, SuperBetter, 68–69.

47.   Steven Kotler and Jamie Wheal, *Stealing Fire: How Silicon Valley, the Navy Seals, and Maverick Scientists Are Revolutionizing the Way We Live and Work* (New York: HarperCollins, 2017), 13–14.

48.   Jackson, *Eleven Rings*, 210.

49.   Hesse, *The Glass Bead Game*, 120.

50.   Sheridan, *The Fighter's Mind*, 76.

51.   McGonigal, *SuperBetter*, 198.

52.   Associated Press, "Novak Djokovic Outlasts Rafael Nadal," January 29, 2012, ESPN, https://www.espn.com/tennis/aus12/story/_/id/7515950/2012-australian -open-novak-djokovic-outlasts-rafael-nadal-longest-grand-slam-final.

53.   Associated Press, "Novak Djokovic Outlasts Rafael Nadal," ESPN.

54.   Kotler, *The Rise of Superman*, 15.

55.   Kotler, *The Rise of Superman*, 15.

56.   Kotler, *The Rise of Superman*, 16–17.

57.   Kotler, *The Rise of Superman*, 117.

58.   Kotler, *The Rise of Superman*, 116.

59.   Kotler, *The Rise of Superman*, 116.

60.   Kotler, *The Rise of Superman*, 117.

61.   Waitzkin, *The Art of Learning*, 88.

62.   Nachmanovitch, *Free Play*, 43.

63.   Gallwey, *The Inner Game of Tennis*, 120–121.

64.   Waitzkin, *The Art of Learning*, 52.

65.   Gallwey, *The Inner Game of Tennis*, 121.

66.   Jackson, *Eleven Rings*, 23.

67.   Jackson, *Eleven Rings*, 184.

68.   Jackson, *Eleven Rings*, 184.

69.   Carse, *Finite and Infinite Games*, 7.

70.   Sheridan, *The Fighter's Mind*, 18–20.

71.   Waitzkin, *The Art of Learning*, 59.

72.   Waitzkin, *The Art of Learning*, 58.

73.   Waitzkin, *The Art of Learning*, 201–202.

74.   Waitzkin, *The Art of Learning*, 204.

75.   Waitzkin, *The Art of Learning*, 204–205.

76.   Waitzkin, *The Art of Learning*, 205.

77.   Waitzkin, *The Art of Learning*, 211.

CHAPTER FIVE

1. Rumi, *The Essential Rumi,* "Inner Wakefulness."
2. Hesse, *The Glass Bead Game,* 81.
3. Kinsley, *The Divine Player,* 2.
4. Alex Johnson, trans. *Diamond Sutra,* chapter 32, accessed August 5, 2023, https://diamond-sutra.com/read-the-diamond-sutra-here/diamond-sutra -chapter-32/.
5. Rumi, *The Essential Rumi,* "Inner Wakefulness."
6. Eric Berne, *Games People Play: The Basic Handbook of Transactional Analysis* (New York: Grove Press, 1964), 76.
7. McGonigal, *Reality Is Broken,* 36.
8. Thomas Lewis, Fari Amini, and Richard Lannon, *A General Theory of Love* (New York: Random House, Inc. 2000), Kindle Location 1881.
9. Lewis, Amini, and Lannon, *A General Theory of Love,* Kindle Location 2166.
10. Jessica Benjamin, *Beyond Do-er and Done-to: Recognition Theory, Intersubjectivity and the Third* (Oxfordshire, UK: Routledge, 2018), 5.
11. Eric Berne, *Transactional Analysis in Psychotherapy,* Kindle Location 1764.
12. Berne, *Games People Play,* 20.
13. Berne, *Games People Play,* 20.
14. Berne, *Games People Play,* 76.
15. Stephen B. Karpman, *Game Free Life: The Definitive Book on the Drama Triangle and the Compassion Triangle* (San Francisco, CA: Drama Triangle Publications, 2014), 30.
16. Berne, *Games People Play,* 25.
17. Karpman, *Game Free Life,* 28.
18. Muriel James and Dorothy Jongeward, *Born to Win: Transactional Analysis with Gestalt Experiments* (Washington, DC: National Geographic Books, 1978), Kindle Locations 404–407.
19. Gabor Maté and Daniel Maté, *The Myth of Normal: Trauma, Illness, and Healing in a Toxic Culture* (New York: Penguin Random House, 2022), 259.
20. Al-Anon Family Groups, *How Al-Anon Works for Families and Friends of Alcoholics* (Virginia Beach, VA: Al-Anon, 1995), 131.
21. Bob Smith and Bill Wilson, *The Big Book of Alcoholics Anonymous* (Scotts Valley, CA: CreateSpace Independent Publishing, 2013), 59–62.
22. Al-Anon Family Groups, *How Al-Anon Works,* 131.
23. Al-Anon Family Groups, *How Al-Anon Works,* 131–132.
24. Al-Anon Family Groups, *How Al-Anon Works,* 131–132.
25. Peter Diamandis, interview with Mo Gawdat, "Are We Living in a Simulation?" Instagram, https://www.instagram.com/reel/CukruAONt6P/?igshid =MTIzZWMxMTBkOA%3D%3D.

26. Nachmanovitch, *Free Play,* 42.

27. Maté and Maté, *The Myth of Normal,* 87.

28. Maté and Maté, *The Myth of Normal,* 90–95.

29. Carl Gustav Jung, *Collected Works of C. G. Jung, Volume 9 (Part 1): Archetypes and the Collective Unconscious.* Gerhard Adler and R. F. C. Hull, eds. (Princeton, NJ: Princeton University Press, 1969), 21, http://www.jstor.org/stable/j.ctt5hhrnk.

30. McGonigal, *SuperBetter,* 149–150

31. Csikszentmihalyi, *Flow,* 9.

32. Lynne Forrest, *Guiding Principles for Life Beyond Victim Consciousness* (Irvington, NY: Conscious Living Media, 2011), Kindle Locations 1476–1497.

33. Forrest, *Guiding Principles for Life,* Kindle Location 1970.

34. Carse, *Finite and Infinite Games,* 74.

35. Stanislav Grof, *The Cosmic Game: Explorations of the Frontiers of Human Consciousness* (Albany, NY: State University of New York Press, 1998), 105.

36. Lewis, Amini, and Lannon, *A General Theory of Love,* Kindle Location 2445.

37. Lewis, Amini, and Lannon, *A General Theory of Love,* Kindle Location 2390.

38. Lewis, Amini, and Lannon, *A General Theory of Love,* Kindle Location 2376–2390.

39. Benjamin, *Beyond Do-er and Done-to,* 31.

40. Ben Harris, "Meet Rick Doblin, the Jewish Psychedelics Advocate Working to Turn a Club Drug into a Legal Medicine," November 19, 2020, Jewish Telegraphic Agency, https://www.jta.org/2020/11/19/health/rick-doblin.

41. Harris, "Meet Rick Doblin," Jewish Telegraphic Agency.

42. Harris, "Meet Rick Doblin," Jewish Telegraphic Agency.

43. PowerfulJRE, interview #1661, "Rick Doblin's DMT Realization About Hitler," 2021, https://www.youtube.com/watch?v=Gd92fg1VWyU.

44. PowerfulJRE, interview #1661, "Rick Doblin's DMT Realization."

45. PowerfulJRE, interview #1661, "Rick Doblin's DMT Realization."

46. Maté and Maté, *The Myth of Normal,* 367.

47. Maté and Maté, *The Myth of Normal,* 368.

48. Maté and Maté, *The Myth of Normal,* 368.

49. Hesse, *The Glass Bead Game,* 82.

50. Carse, *Finite and Infinite Games,* 3.

51. Carse, *Finite and Infinite Games,* 6.

52. Maté and Maté, *The Myth of Normal,* 390–392.

53. Carse, *Finite and Infinite Games,* 23–24.

54. Hesse, *The Glass Bead Game,* 397.

CHAPTER SIX

1. Peter A. Levine, *In an Unspoken Voice: How the Body Releases Trauma and Restores Goodness* (Berkeley, CA: North Atlantic Books, 2010), 2.
2. Kinsley, *The Divine Player,* 187.
3. May, *Love and Will,* 125.
4. May, *Love and Will,* 72.
5. Liz Greene, *Jung's Studies in Astrology: Prophecy, Magic, and the Qualities of Time* (Oxfordshire, UK: Routledge, 2018), 101.
6. Kinsley, *The Divine Player,* 91.
7. Rich Heffern, "Our Brains Are Wired for Liturgy," March 4, 2010, *National Catholic Reporter,* https://www.ncronline.org/news/parish/our-brains-are-wired-liturgy.
8. Andrew Newberg, *Neurotheology: How Science Can Enlighten Us About Spirituality* (New York: Columbia University Press, 2018), 181.
9. May, *Love and Will,* 37.
10. Huizinga, *Homo Ludens,* 20.
11. Robert L. Moore, *The Archetype of Initiation: Sacred Space, Ritual Process, and Personal Transformation,* Max J. Havlick, ed. (Bloomington, IN: Xlibris, 2001), 49.
12. Kinsley, *The Divine Player,* 99.
13. Huizinga, *Homo Ludens,* 14–15.
14. May, *Love and Will,* 138.
15. Vernon L. Scarborough and David R. Wilcox, *The Mesoamerican Ballgame* (Tucson, AZ: University of Arizona Press, 1993), 336.
16. Scarborough and Wilcox, *Mesoamerican Ballgame,* 320.
17. Scarborough and Wilcox, *Mesoamerican Ballgame,* 319.
18. Scarborough and Wilcox, *Mesoamerican Ballgame,* 320.
19. Scarborough and Wilcox, *Mesoamerican Ballgame,* 320.
20. Scarborough and Wilcox, *Mesoamerican Ballgame,* 319.
21. Scarborough and Wilcox, *Mesoamerican Ballgame,* 209.
22. E, Michael Whittington, ed., *The Sport of Life and Death: The Mesoamerican Ballgame* (London: Thames and Hudson Publishing Company, 2001), 45.
23. Whittington, ed., *The Sport of Life and Death,* 45.
24. Whittington, ed., *The Sport of Life and Death,* 46.
25. Whittington, ed., *The Sport of Life and Death,* 46.
26. Scarborough and Wilcox, *The Mesoamerican Ballgame,* 336.
27. Kinsley, *The Divine Player,* 128.
28. May, *Love and Will,* 131.
29. Turner, *From Ritual to Theatre,* 48.
30. May, *Love and Will,* 132.

31. Kinsley, *The Divine Player,* 16.

32. Kinsley, *The Divine Player,* 16.

33. Carolyn Zinko, "Couple Brought Bondage and Body Piercing out of the Dark," September 21, 2017, *San Francisco Chronicle,* https://www.sfchronicle.com/style /article/Couple-brought-bondage-and-body-piercing-out-of-12219467.php.

34. Dossie Easton and Janet W. Hardy, *The New Topping Book* (Eugene, OR: Greenery Press, 2001), 20.

35. Easton and Hardy, *The New Topping Book*, 20.

36. Zinko, "Couple Brought Bondage and Body Piercing out of the Dark," *San Francisco Chronicle.*

37. David M. Ortmann and Richard A. Sprott, *Sexual Outsiders: Understanding BDSM Sexualities and Communities* (Lanham, MD: Rowman and Littlefield Publishers, 2012), Kindle Location 416.

38. Dossie Easton and Janet W. Hardy, *The New Bottoming Book* (Eugene, OR: Greenery Press, 2001), 18.

39. Darren Langdridge, C. Richards, and Meg John Barker, eds., *Safe, Sane, and Consensual: Contemporary Perspectives on Sadomasochism* (London, UK: Palgrave Macmillan, 2007), 225.

40. Easton and Hardy, *The New Topping Book*, 192.

41. Langdridge, Richards, and Barker, eds., *Safe, Sane, and Consensual,* 222.

42. Langdridge, Richards, and Barker, eds., *Safe, Sane, and Consensual,* 224.

43. Kinsley, *The Divine Player,* 161.

44. Levine, *In an Unspoken Voice,* 278.

45. Levine, *In an Unspoken Voice*, Kindle Location 148.

46. Ortmann and Sprott, *Sexual Outsiders,* Kindle Location 1109–1118.

47. Ortmann and Sprott, *Sexual Outsiders*, Kindle Location 1207.

48. Ortmann and Sprott, *Sexual Outsiders*, Kindle Location 1217.

49. Ortmann and Sprott, *Sexual Outsiders*, Kindle Location 1217.

50. Ortmann and Sprott, *Sexual Outsiders*, Kindle Location 1227.

51. Ortmann and Sprott, *Sexual Outsiders*, Kindle Location 1237.

52. Ortmann and Sprott, *Sexual Outsiders*, Kindle Location 1256–1266.

53. Ortmann and Sprott, *Sexual Outsiders*, Kindle Location 1306.

54. Ortmann and Sprott, *Sexual Outsiders*, Kindle Location 1317–1327.

55. Ortmann and Sprott, *Sexual Outsiders*, Kindle Location 1317.

56. Ortmann and Sprott, *Sexual Outsiders*, Kindle Location 1327.

57. Ortmann and Sprott, *Sexual Outsiders*, Kindle Location 1327.

58. Ortmann and Sprott, *Sexual Outsiders*, Kindle Location, 1367–1377.

59. Ortmann and Sprott, *Sexual Outsiders*, Kindle Location 1387–1398.

CHAPTER SEVEN

1. Helen Tworkov, "No Right, No Wrong: An Interview with Pema Chödrön," fall 1993, *Tricycle*, https://tricycle.org/magazine/no-right-no-wrong/.

2. Writvik Gupta, "Top 50 Mad Hatter Quotes from the Quirky Lewis Caroll Character," June 22, 2023, *kidadl*, https://kidadl.com/quotes/top-mad-hatter-quotes-from-the-quirky-lewis-caroll-characte.

3. Joseph Campbell, *Goddesses: Mysteries of the Feminine Divine* (New York: Joseph Campbell Foundation, 2018), 143.

4. Erich Neumann, *The Great Mother: An Analysis of the Archetype* (Princeton, NJ: Princeton University Press, 2015), 299.

From the Author

I WANT TO KNOW LIFE BIBLICALLY, the way a man knows a woman, the way a lover knows a beloved. I want to know the water by getting wet. Theory, commandments, concepts leave me hollow. My driving questions when I come across dicta and dogma are: Is that true? Is it wholly true? Where and how is it true? For whom is it true and why? Can it withstand the test of time? Is it true for me as a woman? The last one has taken me off many a beaten path. Givens are often no longer givens when I ask this question. The world turns upside down. As a free woman, I want all things to be free, liberated from any ideas I would impose on them.

We are constructed of the divine. I believe everything—and I mean everything—when properly tended to, reveals an untold beauty. But my work is not as activist, reformer, saint, teacher, guru, or shaman—it is as artist. Erotic artist. The art I do is akin to found-object art: art made from what has been thrown away. It's an art that turns something back into itself. Like turning prisons into monasteries; the unconscious realm of sex into the spiritual plane of Eros; the degradation of addiction into the art of addiction that isolates the addiction drive for purposes of realization; the life sentence of trauma into human flourishing; the feminism of subjugated women into the feminine collective of inestimable power; those who have been canceled, exiled, and banished into the leaders of the next era; desertified soil into not only carbon-absorbing but nutrient-producing; hunger and food deserts into farm-to-table, free, pop-up restaurants; black culture into the black box for society that holds the secrets. These programs exist, and you can find them here: www.unconditionalfreedom.org.

I founded OneTaste to reawaken our connection with intimacy, with one another, and to the primal source of energy that drives our creativity—sexuality. I created a contemplative discipline around Orgasmic Meditation (OM) that offers an immediate experience of what happens when we unleash rather than repress who we are. Since then, we have gathered some of the greatest research psychologists and neuroscientists to study the intersection of sexuality and human potential in the largest study of its kind since Masters and Johnson. We know that OM has perhaps the most powerful effect of any natural process on healing trauma, promoting well-being, and transcendental experience. I have gathered people and created systems so that the vision can be manifested and grounded in observable benefit.

My work remains as it always was: to turn poison into medicine and make it available to those who want it. But for those who need it, here is the conventional side of things: I graduated from San Francisco State University with a degree in semantics and gender communication. I cofounded the popular avant-garde art gallery 111 Minna Gallery in San Francisco's SoMa district before founding OneTaste.

I have appeared on *ABC News Nightline*, and my work has been featured in the *New York Times, New York Post, San Francisco Chronicle*, and *7x7* magazine, among others. I've written for *Tricycle: The Buddhist Review*, and I wrote the book *Slow Sex: The Art and Craft of the Female Orgasm* (Hachette, 2011). My 2011 TEDxSF talk on OM has been viewed over a million times on YouTube.com.

About Soulmaker Press

SOULMAKER PRESS (SMP) is an independent publisher carving a feminine path to liberation through the use of a variety of media. Soulmaker Press titles and projects are inspired by our five-volume collection of *The Eros Sutras* written by Orgasmic Meditation (OM) founder Nicole Daedone. The Sutras are the essential texts in the study of Eros.

Other titles by Nicole Daedone—ranging from contemporary social commentary based in the principles of Eros, to transformative programs designed for the incarcerated—will be on the launch list. Historically, SMP joins a broad range of ideas and author-led independent, nonmainstream publishers, founded to give voice to marginalized authors and movements. Books are at the core of the company's work, as is collaboration. Soulmaker Press also publishes the newspaper *The Eros Times*, works in collaboration with The Eros Platform—including a weekly Sutra Study program—and produces minidocumentaries, podcasts, and convenings.

Eros, the philosophy linked to OM, is a force of creativity, genius, and connectivity. It animates and unifies the physical and tactile, saturates our experiences, draws us into sensual engagement with other humans and nature, and grounds us in the deepest core of the soul.

Soulmaker Press is part of a group of affiliated businesses, including OneTaste, and nonprofits built around the philosophy of OM. Initiatives inspired by the Sutras are produced by the nonprofit

Unconditional Freedom. That work includes rewilding land, shifting prisons to monasteries that reintegrate the soul, cultivating prison gardens, and establishing Free Food restaurants in San Francisco and New York City. Soulmaker Press will also work with the Institute of OM Foundation to publish breakthrough findings for healing trauma and expanding consciousness through OM.

Soulmaker Press books are available in print and eBook form and can be purchased directly from the publisher and from Amazon, Apple Books, and all other retailers via Ingram. Limited-edition copies of *The Eros Sutras* and Daedone's *The Age of Eros: A Manifesto of Connectivity and Consciousness* are available directly from the publisher.

Printed in Great Britain
by Amazon

37341438R00136